DO-MAGIC
with
YOUR LIFE

How to create and live your dream!

RAI CHOWDHARY

Published by The KPI System
Published in the United States

Do-Magic with Your Life: How to create and live your dream!

Library of Congress Control Number: 2015903405

ISBN: 978-0-9740647-0-3

Printed in the United States of America

Cover and Book Design: Lauren Nadler Design Studio
Illustrations: Erico Almeida Design Studio
Editor: Diane Kimura

Dedicated to

My mother Krishna Chowdhary,
uncle Devdatt Pruthi, and,
my wife Kiran Chowdhary

About the Author

Rai Chowdhary has coached business professionals and executives for more than 20 years at small, medium and Fortune 500 corporations in the U.S. and across the world. He developed the Do-Magic approach by synergizing what he learned, and his experience over the years. It has been applied and tested extensively in business and personal life. This book captures the essence of the applications of Do-Magic© to personal life.

Rai has successfully created and lived numerous dreams over his life, going from a broken teenager to becoming a top engineer – inventing products and technologies that have helped millions. He is also an award winning speaker, author, and entrepreneur.

www.domagicwithyourlife.com

TABLE OF CONTENTS

INTRODUCTION

"Making a buck is easy
making a difference
is tough"

—*Tom Brokaw*

Do you have a dream of what you want to do, who you want to become, and how you want to live? Are you living it? Life provides opportunities, what we do with them is largely up to us.

I have been blessed enough to create and realize my dreams several times over the course of 20+ years. Along the way I have coached others on their journeys. It was at the urging of those, who benefited and saw their lives turn around, that I undertook the writing of this book.

Even when people have a dream, often times they miss out on realizing it for lack of a systematic approach and a framework. One day they wake up, look back and ask: what did I do with all those years? This book provides a solution, that starts with creating your dream, and using the "Do-Magic©" method to realize it.

Each letter of Do-Magic is covered in a chapter in the book, with explanations of what it means, and tips on how to make it happen. The real-life application might be somewhat different from one reader to another, however the overall process should be similar.

Do-Magic is based on the foundations of the scientific method, with added components and concepts from other disciplines such as Project Management, Lean principles, and Six Sigma. Being humans, feelings are an integral part of our lives and so I have delved into psychology, and included aspects from that discipline as well. Much of this book is a reflection of what I have learned, blended, and integrated with my thoughts, ideas, and experiences. With this book, I am giving it back.

I acknowledge and thank all the practitioners and thought leaders who have contributed to the disciplines of Project Management, Lean, Six Sigma, Neuro-science, and Psychology.

Once you Do-Magic with Your Life, you will find a unique sense of accomplishment. This in turn will boost your confidence in pursuing yet another dream. As you succeed, enrich your life, and gain strength—wouldn't it be a good idea to help others do the same, and kindle their lives. I cannot do it alone, and invite you to join me on that journey.

Finally, I would be honored to hear from you; do let me know your comments, what worked for you, and what else you would like to see in future editions of this book. You can reach me at: rai_chowdhary@yahoo.com

Rai Chowdhary

WHY IT IS WORTH YOUR TIME TO READ THIS BOOK

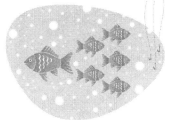

"Success is not final,
     failure is not fatal,
 it is the courage
      to continue that counts."
          —*Winston Churchill*

The future is calling—it is your life—20 percent is what happens to you, 80 percent will be how you respond to it.

With that—the question is how you go about the 80 percent that lies in your hands. What will you do? The future is mostly uncharted territory, awaiting your journey through it, and much of it will become what you make it to be. That leads to questions such as what you want to become, where you want to go, and how you will get there. The answers can come from Do-Magic. As Mahatma Gandhi said—*The future depends on what you do today*. Below I have answered some questions I was asked about this book.

What is Do-Magic and why should I consider it?

Do-Magic is a system and framework to create and live your dream. Briefly, the letters denote:

- **D** – Define your Dream
- **O** – Observe, and be Objective
- **M** – Mindsets, Milestones, and Measures of Success (MOS)
- **A** – Analysis and Action
- **G** – Generate a Timeline and Plan B
- **I** – Implement, and stay Inspired
- **C** – Checks and Balances, Celebration, and Commitment

Life did not come with a user's manual on how to dream or live. The result is that too many people wander through life and achieve far less than their full potential; relying on success by chance. They lose precious time, and wake up one day to find it is too late. Do-Magic enables you to sculpt your success by design.

Finally, like fine grains of sand in your fist, your time on the planet is finite (approximately 36,000 days from the time of birth, 16,000 if you are about age 40). Wouldn't it make sense to make the most of it before it slips away? Achieve something, scale new heights, live for a cause that makes you wake up every day with excitement. You can either count the moments, or make moments count.

"All progress comes from those who do not take the accepted view, nor accept the world as it is"—Neville Goddard

Why bother with a systematic approach?

Let us say you leave things to chance and let life happen. There will be little control over where you end up. You will be like a rudderless boat with uncontrolled sails flapping around in the breeze. Even with the right current and wind, you wouldn't be able to steer it. Additionally, rapids, rocks, eddies, turns and corners are all part of the journey. How will you navigate these? It is also possible, seeing you in such a boat, someone else may attach a tow line and take you to a destination of their choice.

Do-Magic comprises a system and framework that provides knowhow to create your dream and realize it. When knowhow is used in sync with a framework, it can deliver powerful results. Do-Magic enables you to channel your energy in the right direction and for the right reason. Unfocused energy results in explosions that can burn and hurt; only harnessed energy can make power and get work done.

Who can or should Do-Magic?

First—anyone can apply this approach. The results will depend on your starting point, how you use it, and what you apply it to. Students can create a pathway for their careers. Professionals can use it to progress to the next level. Business owners can use it to expand and grow their operations. Teachers can use it to help students achieve more. Moms and dads can apply it to build better families and help their children accomplish more. Coaches or mentors can guide mentees in a constructive manner that produces results.

When to use Do-Magic?

You can apply Do-Magic when you are about to start something new or use it to make improvements to something you are already doing.

Suppose you are at one of life's many turning points, exiting from your previous commitments and engagements. A sense of vast emptiness now fills your life—and the limitless expanse of the future lies ahead. You see endless pathways and trails—each leading in a different direction. You could take an extended trip abroad, go hike the mountains, pursue your next degree, start a business, spend time with your aging parents, or, take an early retirement. You need to make critical life decisions, and there is no text book to refer to. What should you do?

Maybe you are in the middle of a career, and find things are not going the way you had anticipated, or you have gone astray for some reason. Do-Magic can help make course corrections and get your career back on track, or, chart out a new course.

As you can see, regardless of age, gender, or situation, there is a bewildering array of paths one can pursue. Making sound decisions can become so confusing and stressful; some people give up and let things happen. Recall the boat? Rudderless and with uncontrolled sails, where will it take you?

Times of uncertainty are the best opportunities to apply Do-Magic: it has the power to help you focus and move forward, creating and living the life of your choice. You can also choose to do nothing—but the clock will be ticking and time will pass you by. Our wandering mind—left to itself—entertains random thoughts from here and there that may or may not add up to anything. But, it can keep you busy, thereby creating the illusion of progress.

Is this the only way forward?

This is one way to move forward. If you have used another approach, and it has worked—great! If not, consider using Do-Magic. I encourage you to use it, and feel free to adapt it to your needs as you go. If you would be willing to share your experiences for the benefit of others—I will be happy to post your case study on our blogs or website, and with your permission also include it in future editions/versions of this book.

Can you take a short cut and skip some parts?

Do-Magic is an integrated system—as such you will benefit the most from using all parts of it. If you choose a partial approach, it could result in partial success, and in some cases your efforts may be in vain. For example, if you were to apply the A (Analysis and Action), and the I (Implement), you might get movement in random directions; it would be like driving a car without steering it. If you were to use only the D (Dream), M (Measures of Success, or MOS), and A (Analysis)—there will be only thoughts and ideas; but no real progress.

For these reasons, I recommend you study the whole approach and use it as a system. It can truly be a life changing experience and you will never look back.

What about application examples?

I have included case studies of three individuals which we will follow through all the chapters in the book, giving you a complete view of Do-Magic at work. Additionally, there are some examples from my life, other individuals, and one based on NASA's launching of the space shuttle.

What made you write this book and why now?

The system and framework described in this book are a distillation of my learnings from different gurus, and the experiences gained through the application and development of the methods I conceived—both in personal life and business. The inspiration to write this book came when I got feedback from hundreds of attendees from my seminars who commented that they wished they had learned this 10, or even 20 years ago. Many of my students have successfully applied it to their careers and projects; in one instance—students at the Granite Technical School in Salt Lake City, Utah, successfully used this approach on their senior year projects. It was at the urging of these folks that I began composing this book.

How long did it take to create the book?

This book began as I accumulated scribbles of ideas on topics I would want to cover, mostly jotted down on planes, in airport lounges, cafes, and during weekends at home. I accumulated these notes for over a decade. Writing began in earnest in late 2012; however business engagements held me back and I had to postpone writing work until June 2014, when it picked up steam again. Along the way I used 5S[1] extensively, sorting and storing ideas and topics, refining and sequencing the ones that would be included in the book.

---

1. 5S stands for Sort, Shine, Store, Standardize, and Sustain. It is widely applicable, and a practice followed by Lean practitioners on the path of continuous improvement. For more, please see Appendix A.

THE STORY OF DO-MAGIC

"Keep on sowing your seed,
for you never know
which one will grow
perhaps they all will."

—*Albert Einstien*

It was a cool evening during the winter of 1963 in Bombay. I had come back from school and we had finished dinner. My dad took me to the veranda, pointed to a car parked on our street and said, "I bought that car today." In a country where a vast majority of the people could not even afford a bicycle, we now had a car, and we could drive to go see faraway places. My excitement knew no bounds, unable to hold myself back I ran out to see it.

The car was a 1951 Chevy Deluxe—black, four door, three-speed manual—and the license plate was BMU 1274. For some reason, certain numbers, phrases, and events are never forgotten, are they? I had always been fond of cars, and it was such a pleasure to ride in the car with my dad—even today, the memories are as vivid as ever. Through the rest of the year and next summer we made several road trips, and went on picnics with family friends. Life was good.

The seeds are sown
After summer came rainy season. One day we were driving through a heavy downpour and the wipers quit working. Pulling to the side, Dad showed me how to reach the wiper mechanism from under the

dash and operate it manually. For me it was yet another fun thing to do, but he wondered what would have happened if he were driving alone? Then several times in the following months the car would stall on the road, and he would have to repair it on the spot. Fun turned into irritation over time. Seeing him struggle I wondered if I could create machines and products so good they would hardly ever need repairs. That drove me to go watch mechanics work on cars for hours. I would see them building and testing engines, transmissions, carburetors, brakes, just about everything. As I spoke to them asking questions like how things worked and why they broke down, they said engineers design and build these things, and their work determines how good the car would be. My first dream took shape—I would be a top engineer one day, but I had no idea what that entailed.

Then, in 1967—my father passed away. It started a tragic cascade of devastating events over the next two years. Our family had considerable business debt, and the lenders were getting impatient. They warned us of foreclosures, and we faced the nightmarish specter of homelessness and bankruptcy. As if that wasn't enough, I was declared a failure at the board exam in high school. Some of my peers and others piled on physical and mental abuse. By mid-1969, I was a broken teenager, with total loss of confidence in my future and what I could make of myself.

For those of you who have not faced similar circumstances during your early teens, it is hard to fathom; but those that have will understand what it can do to a person—especially at that tender age. I still wanted to realize and live my dream of becoming an engineer and create great products, but without high school graduation there was no way I would be able to attend college. Unable to see a path ahead, and taking a day at a time, I went to work in the factory my father had built, doing back breaking work over the night shifts while attending school during the day.

After considerable struggle, we found the real issue with the board exam; my answer sheet for Civics had been lost, and consequently they had marked me absent. It took a long time to find it and correct the error. The whole episode set me back a full year in getting admission to engineering college. However, once engineering studies started, I never looked back. Energized by seeing myself progress in my chosen field—and with strong pull from visions of being a successful engineer—I topped my class every year and won numerous scholarships along the way. The monies I received paid for all expenses and then some. Not once through these years did I lose sight of what I could and would do after graduation. During this journey I had support from my mother and one of my uncles; both mentored me at different times and in different ways. I went on to get multiple degrees, and created products (auto parts) that became best sellers—we could not keep up with the demand.

Subsequently, this cycle of creating a dream and living it repeated itself multiple times in different settings and places. The products ranged from healthier snack foods to knee, hip, and shoulder joint replacements, and, most recently (2012) non-toxic radiation shielding materials. These products have touched the lives of hundreds of millions by helping improve quality of life.

So—why am I sharing this with you? If you have a dream and a burning desire to realize it, do not lose sight of it. Do not give up—rather, persevere, and relentlessly pursue your dream. The universe comes back with solutions and answers. Doors open that you could never have imagined, and what lies ahead you never know. Opportunities become visible as you move forward. Take the case of Jack Ma, the founder of Alibaba.[2] Known to dream big, he started with essentially nothing, and eventually went on to build one of the world's largest e-commerce companies. He did that by leveraging his deft knowledge of how the Chinese government worked, and combining it with the opportunity to bring China into the digital age. I have seen and experienced such phenomena repeat numerous times. However, I also saw many struggle, and give up. In a vast majority of these cases, there was a lack of the

---

2. Source: http://time.com/time-person-of-the-year-runner-up-jack-ma/

right mindset, or a framework for creating and realizing their dreams was missing. In other cases there was no "fire in the belly."

As I continuously learned over my years, gained experience by failing and succeeding repeatedly, and, mentored others through their struggles to see them come out ahead—a system and framework for success started to take root. It blossomed as it demonstrated excellent results consistently while enabling a richer and more fulfilled life at the same time. This system and framework is "Do-Magic", and it has become my way of life in just about every sphere—not just business life.

Do-Magic starts with you creating your dream and then helps you live it. Regardless of what has happened to you, where you are in life, your age, or your condition, there is no reason why you cannot have a dream and work towards realizing it. This life is a gift, it wasn't your choice. However *what you do with it is your choice.*

Does that guarantee a particular outcome? No—nothing can. But, the results will reflect your efforts—sometimes it may take time—just the way nature does. From seed to harvest for a tomato plant is a matter of months, while a pecan tree or a mango tree may take many years. The tools, techniques, and pointers for mindsets included in Do-Magic make its application easier. The utility is almost limitless.

Each letter in Do-Magic stands for certain core elements and steps, and they are as follows:

D Dream your future and define it in writing. If it's only in your head, it will vaporize; writing it down makes it more permanent. A 1979 Harvard study showed only three percent of their MBA graduate students had written goals; ten years later in a follow up it was found that the three percent who had written goals, earned on average 10 times as much the other 97 percent combined.[3] That is the power of defining your dream. It is what you are working

---

3. Source: http://www.forbes.com/sites/85broads/2014/04/08/why-you-should-be-writing-down-your-goals/

towards, who and what you want to become. Unlike the dream that occurs to you in your sleep without your volition, this is one you create when you are awake and more importantly, with the intent of creating your future—for if you don't, someone else will.

O Observe someone who has done this before, and be Objective. Doing so enables you to move faster through established trails rather than always having to create new ones—which you might have to do on some occasions. Objectivity ensures you will have a sane dream, something that can be really achieved.

M Mindsets, Milestones, and Measures of Success help keep track of progress and provide important feedback. The feedback will include how far you have come, thus boosting your confidence and propelling you forward, as well as what remains to be done.

It is a given that external and internal forces will cause deviations to occur as you move forward; however, the milestones will help in keeping track, and enable you to make corrective actions.

A Analysis and Action. Both are needed to chart out the course for moving forward towards your milestones. Without action, it will all remain empty talk and wishful thinking. Without analysis, you run the risk of taking incorrect actions, and at the wrong time.

G Generate a Timeline and a Plan B. Ensure you have time bound goals and actions to pursue. Laying out a map is essential to see the gaps, connections, and dependencies of various tasks and milestones. A map laid out on paper increases visibility and relieves our mind of the burden of trying to remember everything—freeing up much needed neurons for important cognitive work. Plan B ensures you will have alternatives ahead of time.

I Implement and stay Inspired. Real forward progress happens when well thought-out plans are implemented. It is also true that this is the juncture where intent and reality collaborate or collide—when the latter happens we will need to turn to the well of inspiration.

C Checks and Balances, Celebration, and Commitment. To hold your gains as you cross each milestone, place a wedge so you don't slide back. And don't forget to Celebrate the crossing of milestones; we tend to wait until reaching the final goal to reward ourselves—but that can take time. Finally, a commitment to Do-Magic again ensures we stay on an upward spiral.

In the following seven chapters we will explore Do-Magic at a deeper level using examples and checklists.

DEFINE YOUR DREAM

"The best way
to predict
your future is
to create it."
—*Abraham Lincoln*

D comprises Defining your Dream. In addition, we will also look at other factors that serve as enablers, and catalysts that help set the course. First, let us look at what holds us back.

Check the brakes

Before moving forward to create and live your dream, take a moment to assess the past. Understand what worked and what didn't. What held you back? Was it fear, failure, concern about losing face, inadequate effort, lack of confidence, no vision of what you wanted to become? Or, just plain old bad luck? This is important knowledge and is unique to you; ignoring it will only slow you down, much like trying to drive a car with the brakes on.

An honest assessment of this kind enables us to face reality; knowing the causes paves the way for us to take remedial action—off loading the baggage, so to speak, and freeing us to march forward with courage in a new direction.

Even if you have attempted and not made it previously, do not lose heart. Think of a child: The stumbles, trips, falls, and accompanying bruises are all part of the learning experience on the way to walking and running. Real failure lies in not learning, repeating the same mistakes, and then, giving up.

Below is the chronology of someone's life. As you read through the events, think about who it could be. Notice that "success" only occurs in three of the 15 events.

- 1831 – Lost his job
- 1832 – Defeated in run for Illinois State Legislature
- 1833 – Failed in business
- 1834 – Elected to Illinois State Legislature (**success**)
- 1835 – Sweetheart died
- 1836 – Had nervous breakdown
- 1838 – Defeated in run for Illinois House Speaker
- 1843 – Defeated in run for nomination for U.S. Congress
- 1846 – Elected to Congress (**success**)
- 1848 – Lost re-nomination
- 1849 – Rejected for land officer position
- 1854 – Defeated in run for U.S. Senate
- 1856 – Defeated in run for nomination for Vice President
- 1858 – Again defeated in run for U.S. Senate
- 1860 – Elected President (**success**)

That was Abraham Lincoln.[4]

Each one of us has unique gifts, and the power to create our future; however few really know it, and even fewer exercise it. It is only when we unshackle ourselves, direct our attention and focus, that we can unleash our potential. The din of today's connected world drowns out our inner voice, and the fog of ignorance adds to the confusion. We lose our abilities to live full and enriched lives. Chasing one lure after the other, we seek happiness and satisfaction, both of which stay

---

4 Source: http://www.school-for-champions.com/history/lincoln_failures.htm#.VDoVNPldWSo

elusive and fleeting. The result is exhaustion, frustration, and despair. Therein lies the reason why we need to first understand ourselves, then "consciously create" our dream.

As suggested earlier, this dream differs from the one we experience when asleep. It is one that we create consciously in a state of wakefulness. Making it the focal point of your life and purpose, visualizing yourself living it, creates a powerful force that pulls you towards it, regardless of the sphere of life: business, work, family, religion, or spiritual—it doesn't matter.

Define Your Dream

Ask yourself: Where do I want to go? What excites me? What do I want to become? What memories do I want to leave behind? What defines me? What sets me apart? What makes me happy and fulfilled? What makes me jump out of bed and forge ahead with zeal? What lies at the intersection of my passion, strengths and abilities, and the opportunities I see ahead? A simple way to do this is to separately brainstorm and answer these questions the best you can. My *preference* is to start with the list of opportunities and identify the top five that I would want to focus on. This is followed by culling out those that I feel passionate about, and I can pursue using my strengths and abilities.

It is easy to let life happen, just doing "stuff" day in and day out. Or, to just go with the flow, and keep chasing one distraction after another. Yes, many live their lives that way. It is easy, and keeps them in their comfort zone. Don't worry—be happy, and life passes them by day after day.

If you don't have a dream, I submit you are drifting and might reach some random shore one day. When this happens, as a consolation people convince themselves and others that this was their dream anyway! Beware of such delusions—they lead to self-deception and create more harm than the temporary relief from saving face.

Let's delve deeper: Can your dream be grandiose? Can it be small? The answer is yes, and yes. While it does not hurt to have a grandiose dream, one has to remember the bigger the dream, the more time and effort will be required to realize it, and the greater the chances of disappointment especially if this is your first attempt. Nevertheless, remember Dr. Samuel Johnson said, "*Great works are performed not by strength but by perseverance.*" When I was in my teens after I had lost my father, my dream of becoming an engineer was shattered. The only thing I could think of—for some time—was to get through high school. Steadily and in small steps, I kept moving forward, building confidence and eventually graduating with credentials in three engineering disciplines—Mechanical and Manufacturing, followed by a Master's in Engineering Science (Materials), from Arizona State University.

Many others have faced insurmountable odds and persisted in the face of dire adversity to achieve spectacular results. Mahatma Gandhi, a frail man, did not command an army, and faced the wrath of the mighty British Empire dozens of times on his way to creating the India of his dreams. Eventually, India won independence without the use of arms, or waging a war!

There will be times when your dream has not crystallized to the point of being clearly visible and definable. In such situations it is ok to have Discovery as a goal; something like just going North (a general sense of direction) to study the landscape. It will act as a catalyst that enables you to move forward. An exposure to new and different opportunities provides a good starting point from which you can narrow down using a filtering process by asking:

1. Is this something I am really passionate about?
2. How does this fit with who I am and who I want to become?
3. Do I have (or can I acquire) the strengths and abilities to pursue this?

If you are still not sure, keeping options open with alternate destinations in line with your interests can get you moving forward. For example, a 16-year-old may dream of becoming an astronaut one day. Nothing wrong with that; it is an audacious dream. Big dreams need meticulous planning and execution. The smart thing to do is have multiple destinations within the large dream, and think in terms of a journey that takes you through these destinations such as fighter pilot, test pilot, master instructor, etc. As you visualize this happening you will experience the pull, and move forward rather than get stymied by the low probability of selection as an astronaut, and the enormity of that single peak in the distance you want to scale.

There are those who say, "I don't know where I want to go; so I will stay put," or "If I focus on this dream, I might miss out on better opportunities." Such indecisiveness, if continued for long, only leads to more frustration and missed opportunities. But one must remember, it is only with determination and constancy of purpose that you will increase your chances of success. One day there will be a defining moment; you will look back and ask: What did I do with all those precious years? Did I use the gift of my time on the planet wisely?

If you haven't thought of these things, perhaps it is time. Let the face you see in the mirror be of the one who has a dream, is pursuing it diligently, and taking decisive action.

So, here are some tips and nudges for moving forward. Write down the answers to each question, and put them away. Pull them out in a few days, ask if they resonate and feel right. If so, look for the common theme in each of your answers:

- If you knew you the world was ending in 500 days, what would you really want to get done?
- What if instead of 500 it was only 5 days? What would be things you feel you should have finished or accomplished in life?
- If money were no object, what would you do with your time?
- What work/activities lift your spirits?
- If there were one thing that would make you jump out of bed day in and day out with excitement and take on the day with full force, what would that be?
- Think of the people you admire and respect the most. Now imagine they are remembering you. If they had to say a few words about you, what would they say?

Questions like these help you uncover what is really important, what is near and dear to your heart, so that you can head in the right direction, and begin Defining and then pursuing your Dream, not someone else's. As Kay Lyon said, *"Yesterday is a cancelled check, and tomorrow is a promissory note. The only cash you have is today—use it wisely."*

Finally, check the SAILS you have—Strength, Attitude, Information (or Knowledge), Limitations—and cut the Shackles that hold you back. While some of these can be overcome or compensated for, others might be given. Often times limitations and constraints are a figment of the imagination, and self-imposed. The sooner you identify and remove them the better. You were born to soar, not to stall! Rewards will provide the necessary lift, and remember, they can be intrinsic or extrinsic; the former create a deeper sense of accomplishment—the joy being driven by the internal satisfaction that comes from progressing towards the realization of your dream. Extrinsic rewards are more material and transient in nature. It is an individual choice which one to select; both work, however, in different ways and for different people.

IN A NUTSHELL
Design and live your life by choice, not by chance. Define your dream; and if necessary, divide it into chunks. Define destinations within the dream and begin pursuing them diligently. Look at your SAILS, cut the shackles that hold you back; dismantle, and discard them.

CHECKLIST FOR D

Designing a dream takes focus and courage. At this point make sure that:

- ☐ You are willing to look deep inside to assess what is important to you, and, check your dream and direction for alignment
- ☐ You are willing to work through your delusions and distractions
- ☐ You have the drive and determination to continue to drive towards your dream
- ☐ You are ready to exercise diligence, and take decisive action—including saying 'no' to other opportunities that might lure you away
- ☐ It is a dream that you created or that you have thought through even if the idea came from somewhere else
- ☐ You can live with this dream for a long time to come
- ☐ The thought of living this dream/accomplishing it uplifts you with a warmth like no other
- ☐ You already feel the pull because of the passion and want to start the journey right now
- ☐ You are sure this is what you want to be remembered for by the people you revere the most

It is now time to take the next step: using the power of objectivity and observation. As you do this, keep an open mind because you may have to come back and take another look at your Dream. Thus—you might find yourself in a sort of a Do Loop—going back between D and O; however, understand that you will come out ahead with a more achievable Dream.

DESCRIPTION OF WHAT DREAM LOOKS LIKE

EXAMPLE: STUDENT FROM INDIA (KJ)

D○ My dream is to go to the USA, get my MBA from a top-notch university, and be a world leader that makes a difference in the lives of millions through the use of affordable finance.

EXAMPLE: ENGINEER IN THE USA (PC)

D○ For the next ten years, I will create/work on products that enable handicapped people to improve their quality of life, while encouraging my kids and family to create their own dreams and realize them

EXAMPLE: A TOP RANKING OFFICER IN THE MINISTRY OF FINANCE (DC at age ~65)

D○ I will dedicate my life—as long as I can work—to the cause of eradicating blindness in all people

OBSERVE AND BE OBJECTIVE

"Dispassionate objectivity
itself is a passion—for the
real and for the truth."

—*Abraham Maslow*

O involves Observing how your heroes have achieved their dreams, and learning from their mistakes—rather than going through the grind of rediscovering what does not work. O is also about taking an Objective look, or, conducting a critical evaluation of your dream as a reality check. Is the dream really achievable? You may find yourself looping back to D after doing some O; and that is quite alright. The Do part sets the course; therefore, look at the time and effort spent in the Do-loop as an investment and insurance, one that will save you from lots of grief later. Along the way we will also look at challenges in the form of objections and obstacles, traps such as overconfidence, and, opportunities. Let's begin with objectivity first.

Objectivity

Check the dream you have defined and test it for objectivity. Want to start from scratch and become a pro basket-ball player like Michael Jordan in one week? Great dream, you could realize it someday, possibly. But is it objective given you have only one week? I could have a dream of riding my motor cycle to the moon. Well—there is no way that can happen. There are no roads, and motorcycle engines will not work in space. This is a dream alright, but not even in the realm of possibility, and therefore, not objective. A helpful technique to ensure objectivity is to ask if this is attainable. Will I be violating any laws of nature? Remember, nature has been perfecting its ways for eons. On a relative scale of 24 hours as the life of the planet to date, we arrived only seconds ago; we proudly proclaim ourselves to be smart, but we have a long way to go before we can outsmart nature.

Observe

Once you have ensured objectivity, it is time to observe others who might have done this, or something similar. This sequence is important and it will prevent you from going astray. Learning from the mistakes of others will help you avoid doing the same, as well as the time lost to get back on track. Thus, you will be more effective and efficient. It may also open the door to identifying certain individuals as mentors. Suppose the 16-year-old learns that prerequisites to being an astronaut (dream) are a doctoral degree in science or engineering, piloting a jet plane for a minimum of 1000 hours, and that test pilot experience is preferred. He or she can start early on acquiring these.

Another important observation is to assess the gulf between where you are and where you want to be. Take stock of the situation by studying what might work for and against you (your strengths and weaknesses). This in turn prepares you to craft the strategies and execution needed to close the gap between your current and future states (your dream). Training to be an astronaut may require certain levels of physical fitness, and mental acuity; knowing where your 16-year-old stands today will help create the roadmap for attaining the fitness level required for realizing her dream. Understanding the magnitude of the gap will also prevent you from getting *over-confidencitis*—a disease that is more prevalent than thought. Confidence is good only when supported by competence and cool headedness. *Confidence is the fuel that enables liftoff—overconfidence is excess fuel that leads to an explosion.*

It may turn out that your dream passes the test of objectivity, however, you cannot find anyone who has ever done it before. In this case, there is no existing trail, and you will need to blaze your own. Like an explorer without a trail guide map, you may initially consider defining a general direction, as we discussed under *Discover* in D; this might mean going North to discover new countries, and start the journey with that intent. There will be a temptation to play it safe and wait until you have identified a clear destination; this is fine as long as the waiting time does not stretch out to eternity. Staying put is definitely not going to lead you anywhere; rather it will set you back in time and money. It is better to start going forward, cutting and slashing through brush and shrubs as you go—observing and creating key landmarks along the way. For all you know, as you turn a few corners, the destination might show up clearly in sight down the path. Even if it doesn't, you would be proceeding in the general direction as you had planned. Should you discover that you have gone the wrong way, the landmarks you put in place will enable you to return to key milestones and plan your next move. Think of this as a base camp—one that you establish as you prepare to hike that difficult mountain. Here is an example from one of my personal journeys at work in the 1990s:

Objections and Obstacles

I was working on a new technology to bond porous titanium to cobalt-chrome (an alloy widely used in hip, knee, and shoulder joint replacements). This was considered forbidden territory since conventional wisdom considered it impossible; and I was in fact told by my boss to not even attempt it. Millions of dollars had been sunk by competitors and they had failed to create a useable product. It was also accompanied by safety hazards from having molten metal pools in their furnaces, the risk of furnace meltdowns, and ensuing fires. My boss had himself failed in his attempts to pull this off, and perhaps that was the reason he forbade me from going forward. I recall in one of our meetings he flew into a rage and commented, "Engineers like you are a dime a dozen—you work on this project and I will fire you."

But, the company's future was at stake and a burning flame inside me wanted to create the next and better generation of implant products. The dream was to make a difference in people's lives by pushing the boundaries of the state of the art technology of the day, and find ways to succeed where many others had failed. My source of inspiration was Chuck Yeager—the first man to break the sound barrier and survive. Others had attempted this feat before, however, they paid a dear price. For all practical purposes, it was uncharted territory for me. The force was so powerful that it pulled me towards the dream—risking my job and my career at a time I could least afford to do so. I worked on the project clandestinely on weekends and late evenings, with my colleague Rodney—when no one was around. It was exhilarating and scary at the same time, with both of us running experiments and constantly keeping an eye on the entrance door to the R&D lab.

After ascertaining that no laws of science would be violated, studying the gap, and current strengths and capabilities we had in the company, it was clear I would have to use thermal bonding methods and run the process in a vacuum. So, the first milestone I established was to create a thin layer of titanium on a base of cobalt-chrome. It was a sort of a base camp that could be used as a spring board for the remaining journey, and if things went wrong, I could return here, and chart out another course forward. While the story has much more that followed, including the objections and obstacles people threw in my way, this method worked exactly as I had thought. I forged ahead from this key milestone after embedding it firmly in the path by perfecting the technology to create this thin layer of titanium on cobalt-chrome. However, I had to retrace my steps, come back to this key milestone, and go down a different direction to create a porous coating of titanium on cobalt-chrome. In the end, we had an optimal product which offered better bonding with bone, and a highly wear resistant surface made of cobalt-chrome. Knee joint replacements made with this technology became the company's flagship product, and on numerous occasions I was asked by engineers from our competitors, "How in the hell did you do it?"—and I would tell them to go read the patent! Over time the technology was expanded and used for multiple orthopedic and dental implants.

Be prepared to face objections from several quarters—especially when you embark on journeys that others think are impossible. Many times your well-wishers will cast doubt on what can be achieved. Additionally, many obstacles will come your way; some from deliberate actions of others, some due to random chance, and some created by you unknowingly. Regardless, a healthy dose of optimism, coupled with a mindset of looking at obstacles as opportunities will give you the boost you need at such times despite days when you feel that you are too small and powerless.

If you think you are too small to make a difference, try sleeping with a mosquito
—Dalai Lama

Giving up your dream or procrastinating is always an option; however, it puts you in a vicious downward spiral. The more you delay, the more grief and remorse you feel. You lose time, energy, and the motivation to move forward. To stop or reverse this, envision the outcomes you desire; make them crystal clear in your mind. Then look at the obstacles in the path. Can you overcome these—with a stretch? Or, are they unrealistic—for example: a newbie trying to better Michael Jordan after training just one week in the basketball court. The dreams that are of this kind are not objective, and act as de-motivators. In such cases, return to D and start again.

Some of the elements in the next chapter address this very issue. A bias towards action is a surefire way to keep the blues of self-doubt at bay; even if the steps you take are tiny. We will discuss more on action in the subsequent chapter on A.

IN A NUTSHELL

Objectively evaluating your dream is an insurance you cannot live without. Observing who has done this before, and using them as a mentor size up the gap between the current state and where you want to be. You may find yourself looping back to Defining your Dream again—don't be disheartened at all. Look at this as an investment that will pay rich dividends as you come out from the Do-loop and move forward with all your might.

It is now time to look at M—the next step. Having done due diligence in D and O—you are well-positioned to march forward. But wait, wouldn't it be a good idea to ensure you have covered the essentials in the D and O first? Here is a checklist and some examples from those who have used Do-Magic.

CHECKLIST FOR DO
Check how many of the following are true?

- ☐ It is a dream that you created or that you have thought through even if the idea came from somewhere else
- ☐ You can live with this dream for a long time to come
- ☐ The thought of living this dream/accomplishing it uplifts you with a warmth like no other
- ☐ You already feel the pull because of the passion and want to start the journey right now
- ☐ You are sure this is what you want to be remembered for by the people you revere the most
- ☐ You have vetted the dream for being feasible and doable yourself
- ☐ You have verified that no natural laws are violated—that could put a stop to your progress—now or in the future
- ☐ The time to realize your dream is sensible—challenging but not ridiculous
- ☐ Resources (such as money) needed are reasonable or a reachable stretch—but not outrageous

DESCRIPTION OF WHAT "GOOD" LOOKS LIKE

EXAMPLE: STUDENT FROM INDIA (KJ)

> **DO**
>
> My dream is to go to the USA, get my MBA from a top-notch university, and be a world leader that makes a difference in the lives of millions through the use of affordable finance.
>
> I see myself in the affordable finance field starting 2009 (four years from now).
>
> My estimate of the cost to get there is around $190,000 (including fees, books, living expenses, and airfares to and from USA).

EXAMPLE: ENGINEER IN THE USA (PC)

> **DO**
>
> For the next ten years, I will create/work on products that enable people with disabilities to improve their quality of life, while encouraging my kids and family to create their own dreams and realize them
>
> I see myself starting in this field by Q2 next year.
>
> I suspect I might have to accept a lower salary to break into the field, and it might cost me about $4000/year for the first two years.

EXAMPLE: A TOP RANKING OFFICER IN THE MINISTRY OF FINANCE (DC at age ~65)

> **DO**
>
> I will dedicate my life–as long as I can work–to the cause of eradicating blindness in all people
>
> This work has been ongoing, and now I see myself expanding into three bordering states over the next 2 years. Then I will think about other places.

MINDSETS, MILESTONES AND MEASURES OF SUCCESS

"I don't measure success
by how high we climb,
but how high we bounce
when we hit the bottom."
—*George S. Patton*

M is about Mindsets, Milestones, and Measures of Success. All three are essential. Having defined your dream and completed a reality check, it is time to start cultivating the right mindsets for moving forward and tracking progress. Why are mindsets important? Because—as George Patton indicates above—the true indicator of success is how we come back after we fall. There is hardly anyone in this world who did not (or will not) fall hard, at one time or another— from Mahatma Gandhi to Mother Teresa to Muhammad Yunus, the father of microfinance. Their causes and circumstances vary; but look at the difference they made in this world. There are also millions of unsung heroes who live their lives doing the right thing, falling and getting up, and continue working tirelessly for the betterment of self, their families, friends, country, and mankind. Unless you go looking, you will not spot them because the limelight of the media has not made them into celebrities—but they are out there. A rose is a rose whether it blooms in a jungle, or in a garden. I recently met one who has been tirelessly working to improve the lot of slum dwellers in the city of New Delhi.

Mindsets Drive Motivation

Running a check on your Mindset is a crucial first step. So, what does this really mean? The Mind is a funny creature. It is constantly active, but mostly on autopilot, controlling and directing our thoughts, decisions, and actions. In this mode, it makes decisions or triggers action before we process information—and we end up acting before thinking. While this is needed, and works fine for many situations, it gets in the way when we need to focus on more demanding cognitive work such as sketching out our life plan. Left unchecked we end up doing whatever comes our way, and going off track without realizing it. Typically, we lose focus because of mind wandering, habit, and, instinctual automatic responses to stimuli. To stay the course we need to understand how to manage all three. This is no small task, however, with practice, it is achievable. Let's begin by looking at the underlying mechanisms and tackle these distractors—thus priming the pump for success down the road. It must be understood that the mind is not an organ, but is associated with the brain.

Mind Wandering

Why does our mind wander and what can we do about it? While studying this can be a lifetime of work, here are some introductory thoughts.

The mind wanders[5] because our working memory is capable of juggling multiple tasks and thoughts. A robust working memory makes it easier for the mind to wander, especially if the task we are focusing on is boring. However, when challenged, it can overcome distractions and allocate brain resources to deal with pressing problems.

Let us understand how to manage the wandering mind. There is a strong interrelationship between body, mind, and spirit. The mind affects the physical body; for example, the very thought of a relaxing vacation on a beach can affect our heart rate and blood pressure. On the other hand, the prospect of losing a job can send the heart racing

---

5 Source: http://abcnews.go.com/Technology/daydream-believers-minds-wander/story?id=15982248

for some. The body also affects the mind. According to Dr. John Ratey as new dance routines and steps are introduced, the brain produces a greater number of connections between its neurons, which creates a brain that is better able to process more information.[6]

That is why physical fitness and exercises are a must, including yoga, tai chi, or whatever else suits you. I exercise regularly, and on occasion multiple times a day to stay fit, and also find quiet time to contemplate. Another way to improve mental fitness is by learning new things that challenge your mind. Finally, nourishment for the spirit can work wonders when combined with mind and body conditioning; it helps by preventing and healing diseases. People use different approaches— some pray, some engage in missionary or volunteer work, etc. How will you know you are doing enough of this? That is hard for anyone else to say, but you will recognize it when you see your performance and general sense of well-being improve. Having understood the ways we can build mental fitness, we can combine these with the practice of meta-awareness (or, awareness of what and how oneself is thinking), and regain control of the wandering mind.

Habits

Habits—initially we define them, then they take control and define us. Habits are built over time through repetitive actions, and eventually become automatic. They can distract and rob us of time and resources that could be used to pursue our dreams. Often these lie below our conscious state; as such, it is easier for others to spot our habits. Using a friend or mentor to help point them out is a good idea. Bear in mind that the feedback may not be directed at you, but to the habit itself. Habits can be physical or mental, and some can be very constructive indeed. Watch those that are counter-productive and eliminate them.

---

6 A Users Guide to the Brain, Dr. John J. Ratey, MD, page 361

Instinctual Automatic Responses

Automatic responses to stimuli come from emotions and behavior necessary for survival; they are genetic in nature, and not learned—for example, fear and anger. Both suspend rational thought. They can stop progress completely and cause a lot of damage through involuntary and rapid responses that are triggered by instinct.

In today's world, many such behaviors have become irrelevant, and, you can willfully control them without any harm. To accomplish this you need to understand the amygdala hijack (a term coined by Daniel Goleman)—which is described as an immediate and overwhelming emotional response that we may realize later as inappropriate. This hijack occurs faster than thought, putting us in a fight or flight mode as the body opens the flood gates of stress hormones. Recognizing that the hijack is about to occur, or has already occurred, is the first step in dealing with it. That prevents the hijack from going further, and you can hit the pause button—breathe deeply about five times and shift focus away. Doing so allows you to assess the situation from a different perspective. Over time, practicing techniques of mindfulness or meta-awareness, you become the "seer" of your thoughts and actions, thereby preventing the amygdala hijack.

With practice we can learn to defer action, and stay focused. For example—as I was writing this section, my wife happened to make popcorn. The aroma and sound of popping corn got in the way of my work, I was hungry and simply wanted to dash to the kitchen. The amygdala had taken charge, and there it was—the automatic response wanting to take over my cognitive work of writing this chapter in the book. However, maintaining a state of watchfulness, I deferred the automatic action of grabbing a bowl of popped kernels—continued developing the thought I had and kept writing. After crossing this important milestone, it was time to celebrate, and enjoy a bowl of popcorn.

At one time it was believed that the brain is pretty much set after a certain age; but, neuroscience now tells us that it stays plastic, growing and changing far into senior years. Our development has virtually no age limits. This I have confirmed through interviews with several octogenarians, and friends whose parents have lived healthy lives into their 90s. Take the case of Dr. Christin Choma, one of my colleagues. Her father is over 90 at the time of this writing, stays physically very fit, plays chess regularly, and plans on living forever—despite having been through multiple heart surgeries. Then there is the 80 year old Professor Oliver Sacks[7] from NYU School of Medicine. In an article from New York Times of July 6, 2013 he says "Eighty! I can hardly believe it. I often feel life is about to begin…"

We all have our days, and sometimes motivation just sags for no explicable reason. The pros don't quit during these times—they find activities that get them excited and work as pick-me-ups. These can be anything, and don't have to be connected with your dream. Then building off the momentum from these —and having re-charged their batteries—they get back on track again. Examples of what works for me include playing with my dog, going on a short hike, or having a surprise lunch with a friend.

There is no passion to be found playing small—in settling for a life that is less than the one you are capable of living

—Nelson Mandela

Milestones

Having looked at some ideas on Managing our Mind, it is time to look at Milestones.

Milestones are markers along your journey that tell you the distance you have travelled and the remaining distance you need to cover. They can also be used as reference points along the journey where you made decisions and choices. Thus they can be invaluable as progress checks. If you found someone who has realized their dreams before, it makes sense to have them as your Mentor, and solicit their input regarding your Milestones.

---

7 Source: http://www.nytimes.com/2013/07/07/opinion/sunday/the-joy-of-old-age-no-kidding.html?_r=0

If you cannot find anyone, you will need to create your own milestones; one way to do this is by working backwards from your final dream and asking what events need to occur to reach this point. That will help identify a few milestones immediately preceding your dream—then continue that process, asking the same question for each milestone, until you reach your current state.

Since you will be blazing your own trail in this case, you might lack the knowledge to set all milestones in place. But don't let that stall you from moving forward or paralyze you into inaction. If you find yourself in that situation, keep asking and knocking on doors; with today's connected world, and the ability to reach a vast audience using social media, you will be able to find the answers. Further, as you march forward, paths tend to become clearer. You may end up adding milestones, and making some adjustments, and that is quite ok.

As an example—I wrote the milestones on sticky notes and put them on a wall in my home office during my journey to completing this book. The notes read as follows:

- Skeleton of ideas for each chapter completed
- Writing the seven chapters covering D O M A G I C finished
- Graphics designer search initiated
- Editor search started
- Reviewers for the manuscript identified
- Printing house decided
- At least five editor candidates identified
- ...

Note that the milestones are more like events rather than actions, and focused on the "What happened, or what has to happen." When thinking and creating these, it is important to let the thoughts and ideas flow freely; arranging them in the right sequence will come later. If you are doing this for the first time, it is quite likely you will get into identifying the "How," or the action items; instead of resisting that, write down the actions on separate sticky notes and put

MILDSETS, MILESTONES AND MEASURES OF SUCCESS

them in a "parking lot" (a separate place on the wall) to be retrieved later, re-focus, pick up and continue from where you left off.

Milestones need to be written in a way that denotes either the start of an important phase, it's status, or the end. When you accomplish and cross each milestone, you will derive a sense of fulfillment, which fuels the march forward. What worked for me is to put a green checkmark on the milestones that I had crossed—providing an at-a-glance measure of the progress made to date, and what lay ahead. "Seeing" the progress fueled the fire to keep on marching. We will discuss more on celebrating successes crossing each milestone in the chapter on C.

In case you are not sure about how to distinguish between action steps and milestones—here is an example:

1.0 Skeleton of ideas for each chapter completed (milestone)
   1.1 Identify the key learning points in each chapter (action)
   1.2 Link them where possible within the chapter (action)
   1.3 Create bridges between chapters to ensure easy transitions (action)

See the difference; milestones are events, whereas actions are executable steps. They spell out the work to be done, and therefore start with a verb.

Milestones serve another important function. As you embark on your journey, the path you are on might lead to a dead end. You might need to retrace your steps to known milestones (recall the base camp) and strategize, possibly choosing a different path forward and make another attempt at scaling the peak. Without milestones you will be lost—on the way up, and on the way down as well.

Measures of Success

Many people go through life and convince themselves that they are successful. If you ask them how they know they were successful, they say, "I did this, and that, and that." The real question is how does it compare to what they had set out to accomplish? Without a clear definition of the measures of success, you cannot claim a project or task is completed, a milestone reached, or when you can move on to creating and realizing your next dream. Clearly defined measures of success make it easier to stay the course, and know when you have achieved specific goals.

Having understood the importance of measures, one needs to avoid certain traps when choosing them. Many parameters can be measured and beginners often tend to measure everything in sight. That leads to frittering away precious time and resources on trivia. One needs to measure only that which really matters. Carefully selected measures are magnetic in nature, and exert a strong pull especially if they are in constant sight. We as a species have a preference for goal-directed behaviors, because they provide a sense of accomplishment, euphoria, and release dopamine naturally, which our brain craves. So why not harness the power it unleashes in realizing our dream?

When wrong measures are set in place, it can backfire badly through misdirected behaviors. For example, measuring success only in terms of money drives many on to the wrong path of adopting illegal and unethical means to make money. Remember, just because something is measureable does not mean it is the right thing. Paying close attention to the morals and ethics associated with these measures—how these measures align with who you are, your values, dreams, and milestones—is a step few people do diligently. They default to measuring what is available and convenient, or what other people say is important.

In my case, with respect to this book, the measures of success for each milestone and the completion of the book (the dream) was quite clear. I could readily visualize the bound book, the index, the chapters listed out, and on the back cover, comments from people who had reviewed the book. Each chapter had to meet certain criteria for readability, and be completed by a deadline. I could check-mark each milestone as I achieved it and feel the satisfaction of not only having completed it, but also see the completion of the book drawing near.

Did things proceed as planned? Not at all—several events over the years slowed down work or brought it to a halt from time to time. I had to make adjustments to the plan, set new milestones, and get back on track again. However, the dream stayed unchanged like the North Star; even though there were times when I harbored some self-doubt. This is a fact of life, and one needs to take into account that external forces may slow you down, or set you off course. But, if the course is not charted out with milestones and measures of success, how would you even know that you have drifted? How would you ever get back on track?

IN A NUTSHELL

Mindsets, Milestones, and Measures of Success are like the three legs of a stool. Remove any one, and the stool becomes unstable. Mindsets prepare you to move forward, Milestones and Measures of Success ensure you will move forward in the right direction, do the right things, at the right pace.

Laying out your dream, the measures of success, and milestones on paper and placing them on a wall within easy sight makes it easier to hold yourself accountable, and enables consistent progress towards the realization of your dream. We will see the mechanics of how it is done in the next chapter. But wait—we need to do the check list first before we move on. So, here it is...

CHECKLIST FOR M

You have already exited the Do loop, make sure:

- ☐ You are comfortable with your dream and see yourself living it for a long time to come
- ☐ You can at least see the first few milestones clearly, and have identified them in writing
- ☐ Your frame of mind is positive and energized; you cannot wait to move forward and take action
- ☐ The measures of success for key milestones and for dream realization are defined

DESCRIPTION OF WHAT "GOOD" LOOKS LIKE

EXAMPLE: STUDENT FROM INDIA (KJ)

DO

My dream is to go to the USA, get my MBA from a top-notch university, and be a world leader that makes a difference in the lives of millions through the use of affordable finance.

I see myself in the affordable finance field starting 2009 (four years from now).

My estimate of the cost to get there is around $190,000 (including fees, books, living expenses, and airfares to and from USA).

MAGIC

The major milestones as far as I can see at this time are:	The measures of success by milestone are:
• TOEFL and GRE completed	– Score in top 10% for TOEFL and GRE
• Universities identified	– 15 identified as high potential
• Applications and transcripts submitted	– Submitted to the ones identified on time
• Student visa obtained	– Visa in place 4+ weeks before departure
• Air tickets purchased	
• ...milestones after landing in the US—to be determined...	
• Finished MBA	- Within 2 years from enrollment
• Secured position in financial institution (some time in 2013?)	- Top 10 financial institution with operations worldwide

NOTE: Milestones are presented here in a table, however, in practice I recommend using sticky notes with one milestone on each

DESCRIPTION OF WHAT "GOOD" LOOKS LIKE

EXAMPLE: ENGINEER IN THE USA

DO

For the next ten years, I will create/work on products that enable people with disabilities to improve their quality of life, while encouraging my kids and family to create their own dreams and realize them

I see myself starting in this field by Q2 next year

I suspect I might have to accept a lower salary to break into the field, and it might cost me about $4000/year for the first two years.

MAGIC

Ideally—these are the milestones I will cross:	The measures of success by milestone are:
• Identified which kind of products I would like to work on (restorative, diagnostic, etc...)	– Ones that improve quality of life or save lives
• Listed companies in that field	– At least 12 identified to begin with
• Contacts located in at least 5 companies of choice	– Director level or higher where possible in at least 5 companies
• Secured job offers	– From at least 2 companies within 6 months from start of search
• Next milestones to be created after I join the company	– To be identified at a later date

DESCRIPTION OF WHAT "GOOD" LOOKS LIKE

EXAMPLE: A TOP RANKING OFFICER IN THE MINISTRY OF FINANCE (DC at age ~65)

DO

I will dedicate my life—as long as I can work—to the cause of eradicating blindness in all people

This work has been ongoing, and now I see myself expanding into three bordering states over the next 2 years. Then I will think about other places.

Ideally—these are the milestones I will cross:

MAGIC

My critical milestones are as follows:	The measures of success by milestone are:
1. Deputy is ready for delegating	– Deputy capable of taking over about 30% of my current work
2. Established dialog with local health authorities and hospitals to setup eye clinics in all five bordering states	– Health authorities in at least 2 bordering states by Q2 2005, and top 5 hospitals in each state
3. Selected three states where we will start work	- Three states selected by Q4 2004
4. Work started with 1st. state authorities	- First meeting with state authorities by Q2 2005
5. Estimated funding needs for 1st. state	- Total cost to start eye centers in top 5 hospitals without one
6. Work started with 2nd. state authorities	- First meeting with state authorities by Q3 2005
7. Estimated funding needs for 2nd. state	- Total cost to start eye centers in top 5 hospitals without one
8. Work started with 3rd. state authorities	- First meeting with state authorities by Q2 2006
9. Estimated funding needs for 3rd. state	- Total cost to start eye center in top 5 hospitals without one
10....more milestones to be identified	

ANALYSIS
AND ACTION

"The successful person
has the habit of doing
things the failures
don't like to do."

—*Thomas Edison*

So far, by using the D, O, and M we have identified the What and done some ground work to create track-able points on the roadmap. It is now time to work on the details of the How—to reach and cross the milestones on the way to realizing our dream. That requires Analysis and identifying Action items. Analysis comprises sizing up the gap between the current state and our first milestone, and, the gaps between successive milestones. The outcome of analysis will be steps we can take to close the gap. The enablers for proper analysis and actions are Attention and Attitude, which at this juncture are more important than ever because they have a direct bearing on what we will accomplish going forward. This chapter would not be complete without a discussion of these two concepts so we will visit them as well. As you can see—now we are going from a 60,000-foot view to a 5000-foot, view for a better perspective of the landscape.

Analysis and Action

Analyzing the gap between where we are and where we want to be enables us to get a sense of the resources needed, so we can start planning. Using help from mentors can make the analysis easier, and more realistic—especially if we are in uncharted territory. Sometimes the enormity of the gap can stall us into inaction. That is why maintaining a can-do attitude is so important. It ensures the stall does not turn into a free fall. This is an opportune time for the amygdala to hijack your attention since the true magnitude of what we need to do becomes visible for the first time. Therefore, practicing meta-awareness of our attention is a must as we move forward, conducting gap analysis and identifying actions. Breaking down the required actions into bite-size chunks will help by making near term goals easily achievable, speeding up progress, and creating an adrenaline rush that keeps us moving forward with gusto.

As I decided to come to the United States for graduate study in engineering during early 1980s, the enormity of the task almost paralyzed me into inaction. I had hardly travelled in India, let alone going abroad, and had no clue of what life would be like in the U.S. I had seen some Hollywood movies, from which images of gun toting cowboys and motorcycle gangs lingered in my mind. It was impossible for me to get an accurate sense of what I might face after landing in the U.S. Remember, it was an era when the Internet did not exist, and phone calls from India were prohibitively expensive. Newspapers, TV, and radio were the main sources of news and information, and they were woefully inadequate for what I wanted to know.

My mentor at that time was Ashok Khandkar, a dear friend who had traversed this path ahead of me—coming to the U.S. as a student. With his guidance, and some help from the local U.S. consulate, I could identify major milestones and the actions I needed to take. Still, the whole endeavor loomed large because while attending business school in the evenings, and running the business, I needed to spend time getting a passport, prepare literally hundreds of documents for my visa, fill out and send university applications, get recommendation letters, and make funding arrangements; then finally—make the daunting trip to America. Complicating matters was the fact that I would have to leave my mother alone to shoulder the burden of running the family business all by herself. It was a financial, logistic and an emotional challenge all at the same time.

Using a can-do mindset, I forged ahead anyway—pulled by my dream, setting major milestones in place, and identifying the actions needed. Then, breaking the actions into bite size chunks I could visualize myself finishing off the tasks, remembering what my uncle had said: "You cannot eat the whole elephant at once—so eat it one bite at a time..." The approach worked; I made it to the U.S., and completed my Masters in Engineering in 1985. Here is an illustration of one of the milestones and the actions from the roadmap I created at that time:

- Transcripts submitted to universities (Milestone—the what)
    - Get 15 sets of transcripts notarized (Action—the how)
        - Mail to Johns Hopkins University (bite size chunk—task for today)
        - Mail to University of Minnesota (bite size chunk—task for today)
        - ...

Note that the action items and their bite size chunks use active verb and noun combinations.

Attention Hijack and How to Tackle It

During times of fear and distress, a voice inside might tell you this cannot be done; that the actions needed are beyond you, you are destined to fail, and your attention is better focused on things that lie within easy reach of your comfort zone. You may be tempted to abandon your dream.

But wait! During the Do loop—you went through due diligence, ensured that your dream was objective, and, no natural laws were being violated. So this voice is probably a flight response from your amygdala trying to hijack your attention and divert it to where it feels comfortable. The very act of recognizing this defeats the amygdala hijack before it can launch a full attack. My first experience with this was when I failed the high school board exam in India; that setback dealt me a blow at a time when I was psychologically down to begin with. I lost confidence in myself and didn't even attempt to prepare for the entrance exam required for the top engineering college at the time. It was a time when I had not learned these concepts yet. Later in life there were several repeat occurrences; during my college days in India and in the U.S., and during my career as I worked on inventions and challenges where others had attempted but failed. As I learned how to Do-Magic, practice meta-awareness, persevere, break down the task into smaller steps, visualize what success would look like—allowing the pull to work on me, and focusing on the nearest two to three milestones—it helped me move further along. In some instances, I had mentors who stood by me as during my teen years, providing much needed support. One of them was my mother, and another was a dear uncle.

The writing of this book also seemed like an enormous task, with a lot of unknowns. I knew the material, and lived by it regularly, but the concern was how to verbalize it in a succinct manner. What exactly do I write? What is the message? How will I convey it? Where do I start? What chapters should be in the book? How do I sequence and compose the chapters? Who will help me proofread? Again, identifying key milestones and actions helped break down the enormity of the task, cleared the fog, and allowed me to focus attention on short term milestones and necessary actions—which I could track to measure progress.

Analyzing how to put this book together and reach the different milestones, I realized it would be better to compose one chapter for each of the letters in Do-Magic, and string them together. This lead to the following approach for each section:

- Research relevant topics
- Create key points to cover
- Organize the skeleton, and then,
- Write the chapter, making sure linkages between chapters were also explained.

Attitude

Along the way I went through some very stressful times, so I had to work extra hard to ensure my confidence and can-do attitude stayed positive and cheerful. The work of writing is rather solitary, with little to no feedback so one has to be their own source of inspiration (covered in the chapter on I). Careful life planning and having a back-up or Plan B (more on this in the chapter on G) for finances helped me maintain my cool. Staying focused on executing the actions and reaching milestones unleashed enough endorphins to keep the amygdala hijack at bay. Additionally, the joy from the Celebrations (covered in the chapter on C) of completing each chapter kept spirits high, fueling the drive to reach the next milestone.

IN A NUTSHELL

Analysis of what Actions are required to move forward clears away fog and uncertainty. While you might not be able to identify all the actions necessary, it still helps by shedding light on steps you need to take. Since the mind can wander off easily due to random mental events and stimuli, and cause you to go off track, you will need to practice meta-awareness of your Attention. Besides, the importance of cultivating a can-do attitude cannot be emphasized enough at this critical juncture.

We are at a point where a timeline needs to be created as well as alternatives identified, since even the most well thought out plans do not go exactly as intended. That is next, in the chapter on G where we will discuss generating a timeline and Plan B—but only after we complete the checklist for A.

NOTE: The Action Items list will be dynamic in nature—i.e., you might discover more as you get further along. Depending on the criticality of the new Action Items—you may choose to table them in the parking lot or add them and evaluate their impact to your plan. It is a good idea to say "NO" where possible.

CHECKLIST FOR A
Check to make sure:

- ☐ Your dream is *intact*, and matches what you wrote down earlier—you can see yourself living it, and feel what life will be like
- ☐ At least the first few milestones are in sight and you know the actions required to reach them
- ☐ Gap analysis is completed, actions identified to reach the first milestone, and at least the two subsequent milestones (to the extent you can at this time)

☐ Your attitude is one of success, and your attention is riveted on the actions and milestones required to move forward towards your dream; if there are any distractors, you can manage them easily and stay focused

☐ Resources (such as money) have been vetted against the actions identified

☐ Actions and measures of success have been checked for compatibility with milestones

DESCRIPTION OF WHAT "GOOD" LOOKS LIKE

EXAMPLE: STUDENT FROM INDIA (KJ)

DO

My dream is to go to the USA, get my MBA from a top-notch university, and be a world leader that makes a difference in the lives of millions via the use of affordable finance.

I see myself in the affordable finance field starting 2009 (four years from now)

My estimate of the cost to get there is around $190,000 (including fees, books, living expenses, and airfares to and from USA)

MAGIC
• M ○ A

The major milestones as far as I can see at this time are (and required actions):
• TOEFL and GRE completed
  ○ *Fill out TOEFL application*
  ○ *Send fees for TOEFL exam*
  ○ *...*
• Universities identified
  ○ *Search on the web for best professors doing research in affordable finance*
  ○ *Short list universities that offer study areas matching my interest*
  ○ *Eliminate ones that do not offer research assistantship*
  ○ *...*
• Applications and transcripts submitted
  ○ *Send requests for admission materials*
  ○ *Prioritize based on lowest cost of admission and rating of school*
  ○ *...*
• Student visa obtained
• Air tickets purchased
• ...milestones after landing in the US—to be determined...
• Finished MBA
• Secured position in financial institution (some time in 2013?)

DESCRIPTION OF WHAT "GOOD" LOOKS LIKE

EXAMPLE: ENGINEER IN THE USA (PC)

DO

For the next ten years, I will create/work on products that enable people with disabilities to improve their quality of life, while encouraging my kids and family to create their own dreams and realize them

I see myself starting in this field by Q2 next year

I suspect I might have to accept a lower salary to break into the field, and it might cost me about $4000/year for the first two years.

MAGIC
• M ○ A

Ideally—these are the milestones I will cross:

- Identified which kind of products I would like to work on (restorative, diagnostic, etc...)
  - ○ *Open dialog with Dr. Shah to get better understanding of where I might fit*
  - ○ *Talk to 3 recruiters to see how to change industries*
  - ○ *...*
- Listed companies in that field
  - ○ *Study about these companies—Johnson and Johnson, Abbott Labs, Howmedica, Intermedics, and DePuy*
  - ○ *...*
- Contacts located in at least 5 companies of choice
  - ○ *Talk to 3 recruiters*
  - ○ *Call 10 friends to start networking*
  - ○ *...*
- Secured job offers from at least 2 companies (about 6 months from now)
  - ○ *Apply to all 5 companies for different positions I might fit*
  - ○ *Do follow up calls with hiring managers at all 5 companies*
  - ○ *...*
- —Next milestones to be created after I join the company...

DESCRIPTION OF WHAT "GOOD" LOOKS LIKE

EXAMPLE: TOP RANKING OFFICER IN THE MINISTRY OF FINANCE (DC at age ~65)

DO	I will dedicate my life—as long as I can work—to the cause of eradicating blindness in all people
	This work has been ongoing, and now I see myself expanding into three bordering states over the next 2 years. Then I will think about other places.

MAGIC
• M ○ A

My critical milestones are as follows:

- Deputy is ready for delegating about 30% of my current work
  - ○ *Create brief job description*
  - ○ *Advertise in the paper for position*
  - ○ *Screen and hire candidate*
  - ○ *...*
- Established dialog with local health authorities and hospitals to setup eye clinics in all five bordering states
  - ○ *Start dialog initially with hospitals in Himachal, Uttar, and Madhya Pradesh*
  - ○ *Check their infrastructure to support blindness treatments, and availability of doctors*
  - ○ *...*
- Selected three states where we will start work
- Work started with 1st. state (around Q2 2005)
- Estimated funding needs for 1st. state
- Work started with 2nd. State (Q4 2005)
- Estimated funding needs for 2nd. state
- Work started with 3rd. state (Q2 2006)
- Estimated funding needs for 3rd. state
- ...more milestones to be identified as work progresses further...

NOTE: Action Items are presented here in a table, however, in practice I recommend using sticky notes with one action item on each

GENERATE
A TIMELINE
AND PLAN B

"Lost time
is never found
again."
—*Benjamin Franklin*

G is about Generating a timeline and sequencing the milestones and actions. It is here that you will also do risk analysis to prepare yourself should things not go the way you anticipate.

Generate Timeline

At this point we have identified milestones and actions on the journey of realizing your dream. Details of what needs to happen when, and in what sequence, can now be defined adequately using a map. It is a given that there will be surprises along the way. Having thought through what you will do if things go wrong, and having already created a Plan B, reduces the surprise of the surprise (which by the way is more disconcerting than a surprise by itself), and acts like a vaccine against the virus of failure and despair.

One good way to create a timeline is to hang up a sheet of paper on the wall. Write out your dream at the right end of the paper, and the *approximate* time when you want to see it accomplished. I say approximate rather than a particular date because from where you stand today, a very accurate prediction might not be feasible. From that end point draw a horizontal line to the left reaching the other end of the sheet. Next—write each milestone on a sticky note and place it in the right sequence along this line.

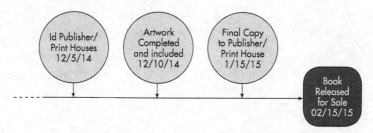

Once you have completed this, stand back, look at the diagram and ask yourself if these milestones make sense. Are they aligned properly? Imagine going through each milestone, painting a picture of what it will feel like, and what tangibles you would have accomplished. Then ask if this leads to the realization of your dream. If you cannot see it in your mind's eye—and on the wall—it will be hard to move forward with focused action. You will need to do this visualization frequently. I have used this technique for myself, coached others over the last 15 years, and on this book project as well.

After laying out the map with milestones, write down the action steps—creating one sticky note per action and place them on the timeline. Ensure that the actions are aligned with the respective milestones. A different shape (or colored) sticky note is recommended so you can distinguish between action items and milestones at a glance. When completed, you will have a road map that lays out step by step what you need to do. Execution becomes easier now since our cognitive capacity is relieved from the burden of trying to remember every detail, completion date, and what comes after what.

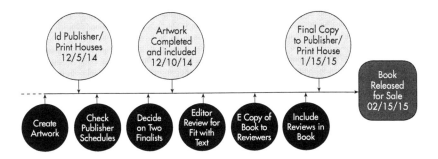

Examine the road map and identify the actions (and milestones) that are non-negotiable. For example, as I was writing this book, it was clear that without a good editor, and a print house, there was no way the book would be a good readable product. Having these resources in place was important for another reason as well—getting the printed copies done in time. Whether I had a marketing agent or any delays in getting one would not hold up the publication in any way. Such prioritization is important since it leads to clearly identifying highly critical milestones. Label them accordingly.

Plan B

The path has been paved to start doing what-ifs and creating Plan B's. In my case I asked the question—if the print house does not perform as promised, what recourse do I have? Do I need to build in a buffer for anticipated delays? Should I check out how busy they will be during those days? How backed up are they? Will I have the funds to pay for the publication? What if the editor disagrees with large parts of the manuscript? Should I be sending her sections or chapters as I write them or wait until the whole book has been written? What are the consequences of each path? How will that impact milestone completion?

This is risk analysis—a sort of insurance. It serves to pre-empt the pitfalls that lie ahead. Granted you won't be able to think of all possible situations, but at least you will be prepared for the ones that you identify and foresee. There are four types of situations that you may find yourself in:

- UNAWARE of what is coming and cannot control the outcomes
- AWARE of what is coming, but cannot control the outcomes
- AWARE of what is coming and can control the outcomes, and
- UNAWARE of what is coming, but can control the outcomes

Here is a graphic to help illustrate the scenarios using four quadrants:

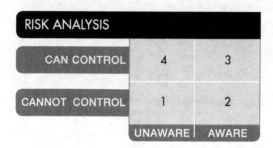

Let us explore this further in the context of how you might analyze risk if you had a family of four with children and were considering moving.

Quadrant 1: Risks that you are not aware of and you have no control over; for example—you are unaware of what regulations are being discussed in city hall that might impact your water quality. This information is likely known to others, however. Unless you make a conscious effort to speak with different folks about your plans or actions, you will never find out about such risks.

Quadrant 2: This quadrant contains risks that you are aware of, but cannot control; for example—city hall has published that it is going to increase chlorine in the water supply. You are allergic to chlorine, and have become aware of the city's action via a notification you got in the mail, however, it is a decision made in the interest of public health and the city will not repeal it.

Quadrant 3: Risks that you are aware of and can exercise control over; for example—the city has sent you a notice that your property taxes will increase by $5,500 the next tax year, unless you prove that the house is your primary residence. In this case you can provide an affidavit that the house is indeed your primary residence and that will suffice to avoid the tax hike.

Quadrant 4: Comprises risks you are unaware of, but can control; for example—the city is planning on opening your street to general traffic, thereby increasing the risk of accidents and injuries to children in the neighborhood. However, you are unaware of this plan. But you do know that according to the local laws, you can stop them from making changes to accessibility of the street to general traffic via a petition.

Of these four, the risks that lie in Quadrant 1 are the most hideous because they are in your blind spot and you cannot exercise control over these risks. To uncover these you will need to lean on others to get different perspectives, and gain insight. Relying on friends and family can help; however, there is always the chance that their input will be biased. Mentors, or other neutral third parties—especially if they don't have a personal stake in the outcomes—would be better sources to help illuminate what lies in the blind spot. Once the risks are identified, steps can be taken for de-risking, or damage control as needed.

I recall the years after I had graduated with my bachelor's degree in India, and was preparing to come to the U.S. for further study. It was one of the most difficult decisions I had ever made—uprooting myself, and coming to a foreign land with no assurance of how I would earn enough to pay the fees and student living expenses. We were not permitted to work while on a student visa, so either I had to get an assistantship at the university, or dip into my savings wiping them out completely. However, I was more concerned about the hidden pitfalls that lay ahead. When I spoke with my friend who was already in the U.S., he assured me I would be taken care of. Still, the decision was not quite that easy for me because my mother was aging, and we had a family business as well. Leaving her alone to shoulder the burden of managing the business was not something I really wanted as an outcome. I had to seek advice and guidance on the steps I should take and create a Plan B—which was to stow away enough money for a return ticket to India in case things really misfired in the U.S., or in case my mother needed me back. Even more important was the mindset I had to create where I would be willing to take such action should it become necessary. It really was a case of holding up my values vs. the willingness to delay my dream.

NOTE: as you conduct what–ifs and risk analysis, you may find yourself adding more action items to your list that were not part of the original plan. This is to be expected. Hopefully you will not need to activate Plan B, and there will be no need for such actions as you proceed—but you will be in a state of readiness—just in case. I recommend creating Plan B together with milestones and action items on a separate sheet and placing it on the wall adjacent to the one you are working on, thus keeping both easily visible.

Risk Analysis

To effectively develop Plan B—you will need to identify what could go wrong. Most likely you will discover many potential adverse events when such an inquiry is made. Much like an iceberg, more than 80 percent of these risks lie sub-surface until they are scouted out. Dealing with every risk will not be feasible, one way to prioritize which ones to mitigate is to evaluate each adverse event using three dimensions: the severity of the outcome, the probability the event would occur, and can it be detected in time. The worst combination is high severity, high probability and low possibility of detection. Conducting such analysis is extremely important for highly complex projects you undertake in your life. We could learn a lesson here from the U.S. Special Forces. Dan Coyle—the expert on 'expertise'—says it's an essential part of how the U.S. Special Forces prepare for every dangerous mission: "…they spend the entire morning going over every possible mistake or disaster that could happen during the mission. Every possible screw-up is mercilessly examined, and linked to an appropriate response: *if the helicopter crash-lands, we'll do X. If we are dropped off at the wrong spot, we'll do Y. If we are outnumbered, we'll do Z."* [8]

---

8 Source: http://thetalentcode.com/2014/01/21/how-to-prepare-for-a-big-moment

Here is a snapshot of the risk analysis from DC's journey to implement his dream of eradicating blindness in India. The following table shows how he went about identifying which aspect of the project carried the highest risk for a given state or region. Factors in consideration were the ability to recruit doctors, permitting, construction, government funding, private funding, and reach to rural areas. Note that the composite risk score is quantified by multiplying the scores from three dimensions—Severity of the effect of something going wrong, Probability that it will, and our ability to Detect impending failure. This is in line with the approach risk analysis practitioners use when studying potential failures with the tool Failure Modes and Effects Analysis, or FMEA (for more on FMEA, please see Appendix C). DC used a simple scale of 1 to 3 for each of the dimensions of risk (Severity, Probability, and Detection), and trained his deputy on conducting this analysis for him so he could focus on the most risky aspects and take early action.

In this case it was clear that for the state under consideration, his priorities needed to be recruiting doctors and securing funds from leaders in the local community (based on the high Composite scores):

FACTORS						
DIMENSION OF RISK	Permitting Delays	Construction Delays	Recruiting Doctors	Rural Reach	Funding State	Funding Private
SEVERITY	1	2	3	1	1	2
PROBABILITY	2	1	3	1	1	3
DETECTION	1	1	3	1	2	3
COMPOSITE SCORE	2	2	27	1	2	18

It must be noted that in the absence of composite risk scores, one would have to churn and mentally process over 18 individual data points (six factors multiplied by three dimensions for each) to comprehend which factor to focus on and de-risk. Research shows this is far beyond the limit of variables most humans can process mentally. [9]

---

9 Source: http://www.psychologicalscience.org/pdf/ps/mind_variables.pdf

IN A NUTSHELL

Generating a Timeline is essential to ensure you have your milestones and actions lined up in the right sequence. Further, laying it out on paper and placing it in constant sight makes it easy to see at a glance where you stand and what you need to do. Risk analysis helps identify what should be your Plan B, or how you should prioritize your work and what evasive measures you can take on a pro-active basis. After all, the best time to dig a well is when you are not thirsty!

A significant amount of the planning work is done by the time one gets to the end of G. Implementation is next, and that is where the rubber meets the road. This juncture is a good point to take stock of our mindsets and make sure we are primed for success. Overviewing the entire game plan at this point before taking a leap forward is a good idea!

CHECKLIST FOR G

The following questions are pertinent and will serve you well before going forward:

- ☐ Are most of the major milestones identified on the way to your dream; or, at least the first two or three are identified and you are working to identify the rest of them to the best of your ability?
- ☐ Have the required actions to reach milestones been analyzed and identified (at least for the first two or three milestones)?
- ☐ Did you lay out the milestones and actions on a timeline? Is it placed on a wall for easy visibility and tracking?
- ☐ Have you identified a back-up plan that has been thought through in case there are extenuating circumstances that stop your progress completely? Is it also placed on the wall?
- ☐ Was risk analysis conducted to identify potential stumbling blocks? Can you pin point the milestones with high risk levels?
- ☐ Do you have a plan to deal with these to the extent you can foresee?

EXAMPLES:

(NOTE: Illustrations below are partial reconstructions of actual maps from the respective individuals)

1—STUDENT FROM INDIA (KJ)

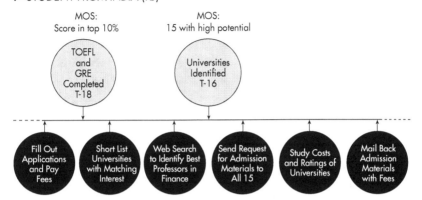

NOTE: KJ used T as the time when he would land in the US, thus in the timeline above, T-18 represents 18 months before. He abbreviated Measures of Success as MOS

2—ENGINEER IN THE USA (PC)

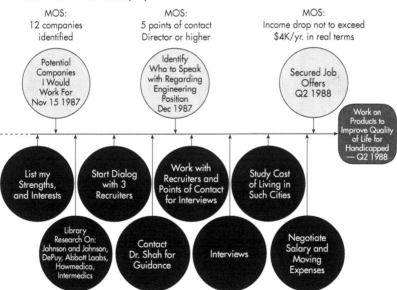

NOTE: All items above may not match exactly what was illustrated earlier in Do and M; that is to be expected since one has to adapt and make adjustments we move forward.

3—A TOP RANKING OFFICER IN THE MINISTRY OF FINANCE (DC AT AGE ~65)

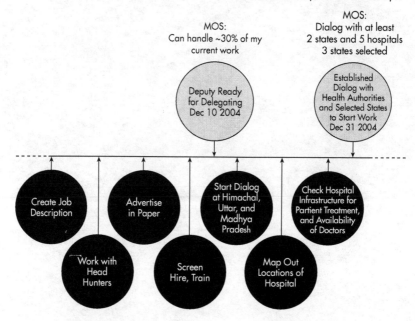

MOS:
Can handle ~30% of my
current work

MOS:
Dialog with at least
2 states and 5 hospitals
3 states selected

Deputy Ready
for Delegating
Dec 10 2004

Established
Dialog with
Health Authorities
and Selected States
to Start Work
Dec 31 2004

Create Job
Description

Advertise
in Paper

Start Dialog
at Himachal,
Uttar, and
Madhya
Pradesh

Check Hospital
Infrastructure for
Partient Treatment,
and Availability
of Doctors

Work with
Head
Hunters

Screen
Hire, Train

Map Out
Locations of
Hospital

IMPLEMENT AND STAY INSPIRED

"The value of an idea lies in the using of it."

—*Thomas Edison*

I is about Implementing and Inspiration. Whatever we have discussed so far has been a mental or a paper exercise. No actions have been implemented yet to close the gap between your current state and any milestones. Now it is time to execute on the actions identified in the timeline. Having done the ground work so far, implementation should proceed expediently and in a much more focused manner. This can be the most difficult of all phases, because now plans and intent meet reality, you will experience periods of euphoria interspersed with grief and despair. Inspiration will come to the rescue.

Implement

It is a key phase in your journey—exhilarating for some, scary for others. Both emotions occur for the same underlying reason—you are about to embark on the journey of your life. Fear sets in because of being unsure if it is the right thing to do, acting like brakes on your march forward. First you will need to recognize that fear is over taking you. You can observe the impact of fear as days pass by, actions are left incomplete and/or focus is shifting to other things that keep grabbing your attention and pulling you away, or you default to what is easy and convenient. Left unchecked, this can become a downward spiral that becomes hard to reverse; therefore, frequent checks in the form of Inspections to make sure we stay the course are vital.

Here are strategies and tips that have worked well in many situations. You can use them individually or in any combination to deal with your fears should they become overwhelming, and to continue to stay on track:

1. Remind yourself—there is a Plan B which you have set in place; if things go seriously wrong and you end up in a jam, reverting to the backup plan can be a way out. Let this be the option of last resort, however.

2. Study the first one or two milestones and the actions required for them—then ask: What have I got to lose if I were to take these steps and reach the first milestone? Will the loss destroy me? My future? My family? If the answer is a yes—take action to manage these risks immediately and then move further. You can also visualize yourself crossing the milestone, and the joy that comes from achieving that first mini-success. I call it a mini-success since you would have crossed a milestone and indeed moved forward. For subsequent ones, the joy comes from seeing that you have momentum, understanding that with each milestone you cross—there is one less left to go, and realizing that you moved forward successfully by defeating your fear.

3. Tip: Use the 5Ws and 1H (who, what, when, where, why, and how; see Appendix B for more) technique to dissect the fear. This will lead you to the real causes which can be addressed by calmly thinking through and taking steps to prevent such causes. As you do this, adopt the practice of meta-awareness to move yourself into being a seer, and "see" yourself. Then ask: What do I want this person to be? A quitter, or, one who can take on challenges and find smart ways to win?

4. If you find yourself getting into a mode of doing things that are off the path, revert to a state of meta-awareness and watch where your thoughts and actions are taking you. The more you practice this, the better and the easier it gets. Ask: Am I being a victim, going wherever and doing whatever comes my way, or one who has the courage to steer where I need to go?

Once you regain control, and you are back on track, finish a few action items on your list. Doing so will re-ignite the momentum. Looking at the timeline on the wall on a daily basis can help as a reminder of where you are and what is next; it also helps set the course for your day when it is done first thing in the morning.

Soni's Career Dilemma

In the mid-2000s I was coaching a young man, Soni, when he opened up to me and said he was paralyzed into inaction. His family was completely against his pursuing a career in dentistry and because of this he was extremely stressed out. Torn between alienating his family and the pull he felt to pursue his dream—he didn't know what to do, and had lost over six months just taking random courses at the local community college. I suggested he try the 5Ws and 1H approach once everyone was receptive to cool-headed thinking. After learning the approach, he met with the family in an amiable setting and posed questions such as: What is causing this anxiety? Where did it come from? Who in the family are the most anxious? When did such concerns start, and why? Finally he asked how he could help them see his point of view and gain support to pursue his dream. Then the full story unfolded: Two of his sisters were the most vocal about his ability to pursue a program that takes years to complete—they had seen him start and then abandon projects too often—and were concerned that precious family funds would be used up to no avail, depriving the siblings of the opportunities they wanted to pursue. They were of the opinion that he would not stay focused enough and this was just another passing fad. The family opined that he would have to demonstrate to them that this field was really the best one for him, and he would not abandon the pursuit midstream.

Soni went through aptitude testing to find the best fit careers for him. The tests indicated dentistry was amongst the top five career paths. Then he drew up his plan for the next five years using the Do-Magic approach to convince his family that he was serious. Quite a bit of effort went into creating the timeline, identifying the major milestones, and the actions that lay ahead. It was a great way forward for everyone from that point on; Soni pursued his dream with strong support from his family.

Finally, can you imagine Abraham Lincoln, Gandhi, or Mother Teresa in your shoes? They wouldn't give up and quit, would they? As the famous quote goes, Winners never quit, and quitters never win. Having said that, let us not discount fear as trivial.

Fear Can Be Conquered

Fear is natural and powerful; it is driven by the survival instinct, and arises without volition. However, our response to it in these situations *should not* be left to auto pilot—rather, it should be thoughtful and calculated. I recall my mental state when I failed the high school board exam. It was impossible for me to imagine getting into the top university in Bombay, and if someone would have said at that time that I would one day graduate with a Masters in Engineering from the U.S., I would have said, "You must be out of your mind." The fear of failing to get admission was so strong that I came close to abandoning my dream altogether. When my mother saw me harboring such thoughts she nudged me by suggesting that I go for a 'Diploma in Engineering' program (it was more reachable than a Bachelor's Degree) first. If you do well, she told me, you can register for the next challenging program. She pointed out that at worst it would set me back by one year. And, in the long scheme of my whole life, this one year setback would be a lot less damaging than totally giving up on my dream. I took her advice, and never looked back.

Interestingly enough, my daughter found herself in a similar predicament after the weeding process from her freshman year at an engineering college. She wanted to give up on her dream of becoming an engineer. The aptitude tests confirmed again and again that engineering was a best fit career for her. Armed with this knowledge, instead of letting her change to a less desirable field of study, I offered her support and assurance, encouraging her to keep pursuing her dream of becoming an engineer. Together, we worked on peeling the onion to understand why she wanted to give up. Asking "why did this happen" repeatedly took us down a path to the underlying cause. The answer to the first 'why' was that her grades were suffering and she was losing confidence. Eventually, we realized that the real cause was the quality of instruction, not her level of interest or diligence in pursuing the program. So we found ways to remedy the situation via tutoring, coaching, and catching up during summer break to build a strong foundation for the following year. She rose to the challenge and moved forward with courage. Building on her strengths she went on to working for the world's leading car manufacturers—Toyota and Ford. Franklin Roosevelt was right in saying *"We have nothing to fear, but fear itself"*.

Tip: Use aptitude tests to determine your strengths and leverage them to tackle your fears and self-doubt.

Timeline Tells You What To Do

Freed from the alignment and planning effort to a great extent, and having Plan B in place to deal with storms that might buffet us, it is easier to focus on getting things done. The timeline on the wall is a great tool to give you an overall sense of where you need to be at any point in time, and the actions you need to take. More detail pertaining to your day to day work needed to complete the actions and milestones can be included in a to-do list that you carry with you. This ensures the major milestones and actions on the map on the wall are clutter free, and clearly in sight.

There are different ways you can organize such lists; one way is to simply have a running list of items you want to finish and by when. Another is to put them on a daily calendar and allocate time slots. As such you can use your mobile device, laptop, or simply keep it on paper. Use what works for you. I have used all methods at different times and for different reasons; these days I use an online spreadsheet most often for the sake of simplicity and accessibility. The sample illustrated below is a small part of the spreadsheet I used as I was finishing this book. Here the action items are cascaded down from my dream of writing this book, and the milestones on that journey.

ACTION	DUE	STATUS	MILESTONE	DUE
Collect raw notes on D and O	5/30	Done	First draft on D and O completed	9/10
Sort for relevancy to D and O	6/15	Done	First draft on D and O completed	9/10
Collect raw notes on M and A	6/15	Done	First draft on M and A completed	9/20
Sort for relevancy to M and A	6/15	Done	First draft on M and A completed	9/20
Collect raw notes on G I C	6/20	Done	First draft on G I C completed	10/15
Sort for relevancy to G I C	6/30	Done	First draft on G I C completed	10/15
Write each chapter	10/20	Done	Full review by RC completed	11/1
Search for local editors	10/21	Done	Identify editor for book	11/2

The top-down (cascaded) approach ensures the action items will be strongly aligned with what you want to achieve. The way I used the list was to scan the open items on a regular basis to ensure that I stayed on track, and check on items that needed action. Having it accessible from just about anywhere I had an internet connection made it easier to stay on top of what needed to be done.

Also shown is a picture of the timeline with the completed actions and milestones checked off to date. Often times the action items on the timeline might not exactly replicate those in the spreadsheet since the latter has more detail elucidating the bite size chunks.

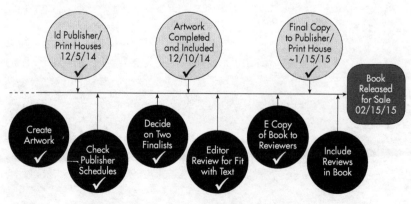

One more thing to bear in mind as you move through the Implement phase is that you will need a good mix of activities to prevent burn out. Some folks can work for hours at end; others need frequent breaks, and then there are those who need a variety of activities. Know thyself, and what keeps you going; use that to leverage your focus any time you find yourself slipping. Self-discipline is a key ingredient that separates the winners from the "also-rans." Just imagine the taste of success and the good feeling as you cross each milestone. If necessary, use some extrinsic rewards linked to each milestone, making sure you wean yourself away and switch to the intrinsic ones as soon as possible—but don't give up or slip on the journey to your dream. This is the only lifetime you have to do it.

As you complete each action item and begin crossing milestones, keep Inspecting to ensure you are on track, and that the Measures of Success are being met. It is a lot easier to make course corrections on any disconnects and deviations as we go rather than going forward and then trying to come back for corrections; in some cases, it might not be feasible to do that at all.

Inspiration and Rewards

With the implementation of action items come the inevitable stumbling blocks. Some will just nick while others will bruise, and in certain cases hurt badly. Despite all precautions and planning, such things will happen; sometimes due to external factors, and at other times due to blind spots we all have. This is the time when the soothing effects of inspiration will reduce the pain, heal, and restore. So let us look at how to make this happen.

Rewards can fuel inspiration; however not all rewards are equally effective. As we discussed earlier, there are two kinds of rewards, extrinsic and intrinsic, and there is a time and place for both. It is here that you may find some extrinsic rewards being more effective in the short term to alleviate the pain. As soon as the pain is in control, switching to intrinsic rewards can work like magic. One of the biggest rewards for me is to see progress towards realizing my dream, and an increasing number of actions showing "done." When I compare that to where I was a few weeks or months ago—it is extremely gratifying, and fuels the fire to continue the march forward despite the bruises. I wish I had known about intrinsic and extrinsic rewards and how to leverage them when I was in my teens. Well, better late than never; and now I have the privilege of sharing it with you.

IN A NUTSHELL

Implementation can be a difficult phase on your journey—because this is where reality meets plans. It is rare that plans will proceed exactly as envisioned. Therefore a will of steel, Inspiration and constant inspection of progress are important elements that need to be deployed in this phase. Implementation can also bring much joy from seeing yourself get closer to realizing your dream, and that can be the catalyst to release energy you may not even know you had.

One of the biggest risks that will start surfacing now is regression. How to hold on to the hard won gains is what we will discuss in the next chapter, but not before we complete the checklist for this phase.

CHECKLIST FOR I

For a phase that begins to deliver results by crossing milestones the following checks are critical:

- ☐ Required actions to reach milestones have been analyzed and identified (at least for the first two or three milestones)
- ☐ You have created to-do lists linked to your actions and milestones—these contain bite size chunks of activity you need to do on a daily basis
- ☐ Meta-awareness is easy for you to practice frequently and you are able to use it to stay focused
- ☐ It is routine for you to focus on your directional vector on a daily basis
- ☐ When work on actions get stuck, you use techniques to find what can be done to begin moving again rather than give up and go do something else
- ☐ Fears have been identified and dealt with appropriately as they occur
- ☐ It is a habit to "inspect" your progress, comparing actual performance against the MOS's for milestones rather than leaving them for later

EXAMPLES

(NOTE: Notice check marks added to completed items)

1—STUDENT FROM INDIA (KJ)

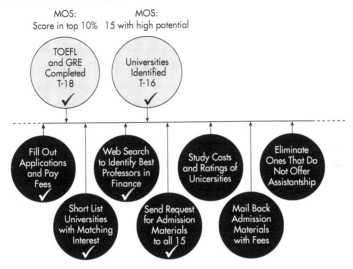

2—ENGINEER IN THE USA (PC)

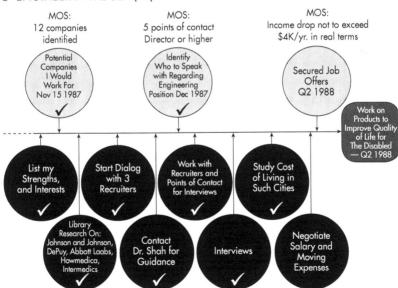

3—A TOP RANKING OFFICER IN THE MINISTRY OF FINANCE (DC AT AGE ~65)

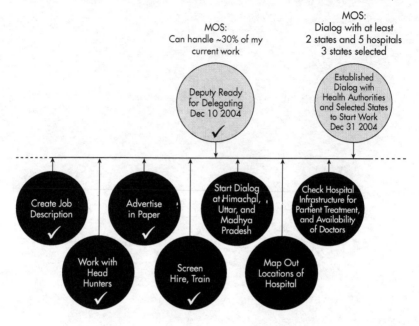

MOS:
Can handle ~30% of my
current work

MOS:
Dialog with at least
2 states and 5 hospitals
3 states selected

Deputy Ready
for Delegating
Dec 10 2004
✓

Established
Dialog with
Health Authorities
and Selected States
to Start Work
Dec 31 2004

Create Job
Description
✓

Advertise
in Paper
✓

Start Dialog
at Himachal,
Uttar, and
Madhya
Pradesh

Check Hospital
Infrastructure for
Partient Treatment,
and Availability
of Doctors

Work with
Head
Hunters
✓

Screen
Hire, Train
✓

Map Out
Locations of
Hospital

CHECKS AND BALANCES, CELEBRATION, AND COMMITMENT

"After climbing a great hill, one only finds there are more hills to climb."

—*Nelson Mandela*

C is about putting Checks and Balances in place to hold your gains, Celebrating the crossing of milestones, and Commitments you make when you start living your dream. There is no clear demarcation point at which the "I" phase ends and "C" starts; you will alternate between the two, or execute them close to each other. While you will get knocks in the implementation phase, you will also bounce back as you rejuvenate yourself with inspiration. The gains are hard won, and practicing the elements in C will keep your momentum steered in the right direction.

Checks and Balances

When in the thick of implementing action items to reach upcoming milestones, the flurry of activity can be very absorbing, and blind us to critical details that warrant attention. The momentum and sense of urgency can override the attention one needs to pay to the Measures of Success (MOS) for the upcoming milestones. I have seen people miss checking against these, or in some cases ignore the MOS, and proceed further for one reason or another. The trouble is that discovering and trying to remedy such misses at a later stage can be difficult to say the least, and in certain situations take you past the point of no return. Take NASA as an example; few organizations are as meticulous in planning out projects as NASA. The launching of a space shuttle involves detailed countdowns, milestones, checks and balances, including technical parameters such as temperatures during launch time, and cloud conditions. On the fateful day of January 28, 1986, temperatures at the time of launch were record lows, and 15 degrees colder than any previous launch.[10] These levels were much below recommended. Yet, a decision was made to launch and the mission was lost due to the disintegration of the shuttle 73 seconds into its journey. Several inquiries were subsequently conducted to determine the causes and make amends, but the fact is—all crew members lost their lives, and the space program suffered a significant setback.

If you were to learn lessons from this event, and think which of the Do-Magic principles were violated, two stand out: Observe, and Measures of Success. This type of pre-launch condition had never been encountered before. And, the "go" milestone violated the minimum criteria for launch temperature. One could argue that hind sight is 20/20; however, I submit that that is a lame way to save face. Trying to argue away in this manner only serves to shift blame, absolve ourselves, and deprives us of learning from our mistakes.

Prevent Regression

Once the MOS for a particular milestone is met, and you move further, it is a good idea to put a wedge at that milestone so that you will not regress past it if you happen to slide back for some reason. That is a way to ensure forward progress is not lost.

Here are some examples from my recent past. My friend Dr. Ashok Khandkar and I were considering the start of a new company in Salt Lake City, Utah, to produce medical products. Two of the major milestones on the journey were *feasibility of technology demonstrated,* and *funding obtained.* The associated MOS's were: (a) cadaver stud-

---

10. Source: http://www.accuweather.com/en/outdoor-articles/astronomy/weather-history-challenger-dis/60648

ies prove the product works, and (b) venture capital firm agrees to fund the first 18 months of operation with intent of funding another round based on our performance. Once these MOS's were achieved, I wound up my training and consulting business in Austin, Texas, and relocated, thus placing a wedge to prevent regression. The new company became my prime focus for the next four years. We faced severe challenges in the new business, including a possible shut down due to a strangle hold by one of our suppliers and the FDA initially declining to clear our flagship product, but for me there was no turning back. The wedge had taken hold. So, we found solutions, innovated, labored smart and hard to get products to market. The company broke several records—producing the world's first radiation blocking cream, toxic metal free radiation shields, and machine washable radiation shielding garments.

Celebrate Crossing the Milestones

While many argue that we should celebrate only after having fully realized our dream, I suggest we should not wait that long. What if the dream is on a long timeline? Challenges of the I phase and the prior work can drain our well of inspiration which is vital fuel in our journey. So, to determine which is more important—feeling good, or, feeling accomplished—I ran a Google query on December 1st, 2014. It returned 83 million hits for "feeling good" vs. 40.6 million for "feeling accomplished. " Just for the sake of comparison, I also queried on "feeling rich;" it returned only 42.4 million hits. If feeling good is so important, then why not have some celebrations along the way to realizing our dream? A good way to do this is celebrate crossing of milestones, especially the major ones.

We can also look at this from the angle of Maslow's hierarchy of needs. There are five discernable levels as shown on next page::

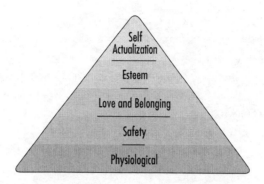

My experience tells me that there is overlap and these can co-exist across the levels. I have seen people trying to meet their physiological needs, and exhibit a certain level of esteem needs as well. Also, the further along one goes in this hierarchy, the less is the need for extrinsic rewards.

Although extrinsic rewards can be quite fulfilling after we reach and cross milestones, a deeper sense of fulfillment might stay elusive. Therefore, extrinsic rewards should be used carefully. I prefer to treat myself or the people I work with using extrinsic rewards only once in a while after accomplishing a major chunk on the timeline. The struggle and effort to earn it makes it richer, and fills the well of inspiration before it runs out. Other than that, much satisfaction comes from the joy of seeing a job well done. The wins for me are reinforced by working on projects of my choice and joining groups where I can meet and expand my horizons in directions I plan to pursue. This happens to be in line with the Self Determination Theory (SDT) as proposed by Dr. Ed Deci and Dr. Rich Ryan (recognized amongst the top 30 education professionals for 2014). According to SDT there are three innate psychological needs that if satisfied lead to optimal performance; they are—(i) competence (ii) autonomy, and (iii) relatedness. Together they act as powerful energizers on your journey of realizing your dream. I recommend that you take time to integrate them with your reward system.

Commitments

Reaching and living your dream will fill you with the joy of your life like no other. The feeling will mimic having climbed a mountain and reached the peak. Enjoy the view as you experience the serenity, the sights of the land below, the fresh air, the clouds, and the nature that surrounds you. Once you have recovered from the fatigue, you will find yourself re-energized and ready to take on the next challenge. Your passion and strengths will be at a new high; however, if you have not created a new dream you will begin to experience a gnawing sense of emptiness. It will be even more pronounced if you have conditioned yourself to achieve new heights using intrinsic rewards.

This is prime time to create another dream and pursue it relentlessly with Do-Magic again. If the whole experience has enriched your life, made you stronger, been rewarding for you, then why not make another commitment—one that could help make this world a better place—by sharing what you have learnt, and helping others live their dream. If the outcomes are not as expected, then it is time to look for reasons why, make Corrections, learn lessons, and Commit to Do-Magic again.

IN A NUTSHELL
Checks and balances, and the use of the wedge to prevent regression are power-ful techniques to ensure you stay on track and do not lose your gains. While the wedge can be a hard thing for many to do, it creates a mindset that the only path is forward. If for some reason, you find it is totally impossible to proceed forward after starting your journey, you can activate Plan B—which will still be a win!

Celebrate along the way to ensure your well of inspiration stays filled, and con-tinues to provide vital nourishment needed on the journey. Take time, hit the pause button after you cross major milestones, look back at the distance you have covered, and the fact that you have moved closer to the realization of your dream. If you are in the early part of the journey and the rest of it seems daunting, con-sider the fact that you are on an important mission of your life, you have done the diligence, and put Plan B in place. So move forward with courage. Edison failed thousands of times before he created the light bulb.

CHECKLIST FOR C

If I were in your shoes at this point, here are checks I would be doing:

- ☐ I have identified and put in place means of celebration (using both intrinsic and some extrinsic rewards) tied to critical milestones, and their respective MOS's

- ☐ I check on progress regularly and ensure it is on track with my plan, correcting deviations when they occur before it is too late

- ☐ I use the wedge as a means to prevent regression and have applied it —especially at critical milestones I have crossed

- ☐ I am committed to having another dream, continuously learning, and helping others reach their dreams

Let us take a look at how the individuals referred to in the book, and a few others, fared on their journeys as they used Do-Magic:

KJ— The student from India completed his MBA from a top 10 business school in the USA, and joined one of the big 5 consulting companies to gain broader experience in finance and operations

PC— The engineer in the U.S. went on to create several medical devices for the benefit of millions

DC— The top ranking officer from the Ministry of Finance helped eradicate blindness for over 100,000 people in India, and established eye clinics in hospitals in three states

Students at the Granite Technical School used this approach on a school project and created a bio reactor for their science competition

My daughter went on to work at Toyota, and then at Ford Motor Company as a design engineer instead of giving up on her dream

Soni became a dental assistant; has made a commitment to create his next dream and progress further in his career

For me—the completion of this book and coaching others on how to Do-Magic in their lives is the realization of yet another dream; now I am in the process of creating my next one. I look forward to the honor of hearing about yours.

PUTTING IT ALL TOGETHER

Make your circumstances, or they will make you
—*Adapted from George Bernard Shaw*

Time is like grains of fine sand. No matter how tightly we hold it in our fist, it slips away. But, it can be turned into a spectacular piece of art if we know how to moisten it right, have a dream of what to create, and know how to sculpt it. So it is with life—it comprises moments and the actions (both physical and mental) we do during those moments. The future is unchartered territory; there are places to go, and paths to get there. There is also raw beauty that can be shaped much like a sculptor creating art from sand on a beach. It can be done with imagination, focus, passion, and a disciplined approach. The system and framework of Do-Magic helps you do just that, so let us reflect and visit the key points from each step.

D: Define your Dream Create a dream and define it by putting it on paper—you can simply write it, or draw it out, or do both. Ensure it is something you are passionate about, have (or are willing to acquire) the strength and ability to achieve it, and there is an opportunity to pursue it.

O: Observe and be Objective Observe who has done this or something similar before, and learn from them. Make sure your dream is objective and achievable.

NOTE: If you find your dream is not objective—you may need to define your dream again

If you cannot find anyone who has done this before, you might be a trail blazer; brace yourself for challenges. Your forward march might need to start with smaller steps, and you will be creating a new path as you go.

M: Mindsets, Milestones, and Measures of Success Mind plays a big role in everything we do, as such learn how to practice meta-awareness; it will pay rich dividends in every walk of life. Milestones are markers on your journey—they might be left by someone who has already been down the path, or you will be creating your own. In either case, they help stay the course, and provide vital feedback on progress. You can also consider milestones to be goals leading up to your dream. Measures of Success are metrics associated with your dream and also cascaded down to milestones. When these are achieved, you can say you crossed that milestone successfully.

A: Analysis and Action Actions happen every moment of the day—physically or mentally, and they are inextricably linked to time. Like loose grains of sand they can slip away, but when tightly bound to your milestones and oriented towards achieving your dream, actions deliver spectacular results. Analysis helps to identify what actions are needed to reach milestones.

G: Generate a Timeline and Plan B Dreams and goals that are not time bound are like wishful thinking—which creates an illusory world. When reality sets in, there is little more than frustration and despair. It is only when you set your dreams and milestones on a timeline that a path starts to emerge. Creating a Plan B is a good idea, especially in cases where several milestones may be at the mercy of the elements, or, carry high uncertainty.

I: Implement and stay Inspired Without implementing action items there will be no progress; however as the saying goes, *all plans are perfect until the first shot is fired*. This part of the journey will bring more euphoria from successes, and despair from knocks. To re-energize and get back on course, you will need to turn to your well of inspiration. Be pro-active and keep it from going dry.

C: Checks and Balances, Celebration, and Commitment Conducting checks regularly to track progress, and comparing actual performance against measures of success ensures you do not go off track. Celebrating when you achieve critical milestones fills the well of inspiration and replenishes the psychological fuel tank. Take a moment to balance yourself, prevent regression, and move forward. Once you have realized your dream, the sense of accomplishment and the accompanying joy will be without parallel. At the same time, there will be a sense of emptiness. Imagine how far you can go if you created your next dream and put the new strengths to work. That requires commitment.

Contagions are rarely beneficial, but this one is different; it eradicates the disease of despair, it can uplift the spirits of millions, and bring cheer to their lives. I cannot do it alone. Would you please join me in this journey by sharing your experiences and stories? I will include them in my books and blogs for the benefit of all.

Finally, I wish you the best in your life's journey, and look forward to hearing from you. You can reach me at rai_chowdhary@yahoo.com

APPENDIX A

5S

The term 5S represents five Japanese words: Seiri, Seiton, Seiro, Seiketru, Shitsuke. In simple English these translate roughly to: Sort, Store, Shine, Standardize, and Sustain. Taken together these actions can help one get organized and to be more effective and efficient in whatever they do. 5S was initially used in manufacturing as part of Lean and other continuous improvement efforts, however, the approach is very useful in personal life as well; whether it is your garage, icons on your desktop, projects you are pursuing, stocks in your portfolio, or anything else. I will share some thoughts on how I applied 5S to the work of writing this book. Let's explore the specifics in each of the S's:

Sort

Sort comprises segregating what is useful and what is not. If you look around you will find plenty of things that are not necessary; they might be surplus, defective, past their useful life, or simply because situations have changed they have become redundant to the current project. Getting rid of these things reduces clutter, and allows you to focus on what is really important.

Over the years I had accumulated hundreds of notes and scribbles, some for my books, others for use in seminars. Applying 5S to these helped ferret out the ones that were relevant for this book. It started with Sort, and asking the question for each note: Does this fit with the theme of this book?

Store

Store involves putting things in their place. There should be a place for everything and everything needs to be in its place. This makes it easy to find things and eliminates the time we waste looking for lost things. For the book, I created files for each chapter and slotted the notes accordingly. This was done for the paper notes, as well as those that were scattered across multiple computers.

The book project would also involve working with multiple editors, artists, reviewers, graphics designers, website developers, and several others. So I created a simple but effective filing system to store the e-mails and electronic files in the right place.

Shine

Shine requires one to clean what they have; it serves multiple purposes: (i) makes things tidy, and (ii) as you clean you inspect. This provides an opportunity to do preventive maintenance, spot discrepancies, and identify problems early.

As far as this book was concerned, Shine involved polishing the notes, and the verbiage in the same to fit the themes and examples in the respective chapters.

Standardize

In Standardize, one makes sure there is a standard way of doing things, including the first three Ss. Doing so boosts efficiency and consistency in results. It also frees up our minds to be more creative for the larger things in life.

Over the course of writing this book, thousands of e-mails were exchanged across the world. Some were for this book, others pertained to previous projects and activities I had been involved with. It could have become messy and very time consuming for me to keep track of who sent me what, why, and when. Adopting simple standardization techniques for file folders, naming conventions, dedicating a separate computer for the writing of the book, and the use of the first three S's helped maintain sanity.

Sustain

Doing the first four S's takes you to a point where things work easier and smoother. However, without conscious effort to sustain this state by doing the above four S's on a regular basis, the gains can be lost. Integrating 5S in our work lays the foundation for excellence in whatever we do.

APPENDIX B
5Ws and 1H

The 5Ws (Who, What, Where, When, and Why) and 1H (How) were originally conceived by Rudyard Kipling as he worked on creating stories. It is a great technique to gather information on just about any topic. I typically select or create questions to ask from the ones listed below. You could come up with more for your use as well.

* *Who is this for?*
* *Who was involved?*
* *Who is asking...*
* *Who is coming?*
* *Who is the customer vs. payer?*
* *Who was there?*
* *Who needs to know?*
* *Who knows about...*
* *Who has done this before?*

* *What exactly does this mean?*
* *What is going on here?*
* *What do we already know about this?*
* *What are the assumptions?*
* *What would happen if ... ?*
* *What is your dream/objective?*
* *What will it cost?*
* *What are the deliverables?*
* *What is needed?*
* *What does success look and feel like?*
* *What does good look like?*
* *What would "your hero" do?*

* *Where did you see/find that?*
* *Where are we going?*
* *Where is the money?*
* *Where did this happen?*
* *Where were you at that time?*
* *Where is it located?*

- *Where did we come from?*
- *Where will this end?*
- *Where have I seen this before?*

- *When did this happen?*
- *When was this planned?*
- *When did you check last time?*
- *When will you...*
- *When is it expected?*
- *When should we...*
- *When will it start/end?*
- *When will I know?*

- *Why did this happen?*
- *Why did we not...*
- *Why was...*
- *Why are we doing this?*
- *Why did we...*
- *Why should I...*

- *How did this happen?*
- *How much did it cost?*
- *How will we...*
- *How did you create your dream?*
- *How to say...*
- *How can we...*
- *How does it affect...*
- *How does this feel?*
- *How about doing...*
- *How would "your hero" do this?*

APPENDIX C

Failure Modes and Effects Analysis (FMEA)

FMEA is a tool to study known and potential failures, their causes and effects, and quantify risk levels. As such, it is frequently used to evaluate risks associated with what can go wrong. Originally used for understanding and analyzing military systems, its use has spread far and wide. It can also be very useful in personal life; my daughter learned the technique and used it for important decisions as she purchased her first car.

Studying Risk in Three Dimensions

Many think of risk being associated with how severe or grave a danger is. As such, they tend to think only in terms of the grossness of the harm that could occur from something going wrong. This is a rather myopic view.

There are myriad events that cause severe harm over time, without any single event causing waves. For example, since the loss of life on a per event basis with auto accidents is lower, it appears less severe than an air crash. However, the frequency of auto accidents is much higher, thus the total loss of life in road travel far exceeds that from air travel. Further, because people don't fly airplanes, they cannot detect an impending event, whereas in the case of a car, they can better detect and try evasive actions. This leads many people to believe that traveling by airplane is more risky than traveling in a car. However, facts show otherwise. FMEA helps by introducing more rationality via the use of three dimensions: severity, frequency, and detection.

Thus, risk is quantified by scoring an event for Severity, Occurrence, and Detection, and multiplying the scores to produce one single number that represents the composite risk.

Here are simple steps on how an FMEA can be applied in personal life:

1. Decide the object of analysis; this can be your project, a product you use, a process for doing something, or milestones on the road map to living your dream

2. Identify things what can go wrong with this object, treating each one as a failure mode (FM). For example, DC applied it to his dream of eradicating blindness in India. As he studied the milestones, and the actions required to achieve them, he identified six FMs that could hamper progress in just about every state: (i) Permitting delays, (ii) Construction delays, (iii) Lack of doctors, (iv) Limited rural reach, (v) Lack of funding by government, and (vi) Lack of funding by individuals or businesses. These FMs could repeat from state to state, although the composite risk from each FM could vary from one state to another

3. Think in terms of three dimensions (Severity, Occurrence, and Detection) for each failure mode. Setup a scoring scale such that higher scores are indicative of higher risk. For example, a scale that has three levels (High, Medium, and Low) would show as follows:

SCORING TABLE		SCORE
SEVERITY OF THE FM	High	3
	Medium	2
	Low	1
PROBABILITY (chances the FM would occur)	High	3
	Medium	2
	Low	1
DETECTION (ease of detection)	Very difficult or impossible to detect	3
	Somewhat difficult to detect	2
	Easy or readily evident	1

4. Evaluate each FM using the three dimensions. For example, DC would ask: How severe would be the consequence of permitting delays in this state? What is the probability that we will see permitting delays? And, How difficult is it to know (or detect) that permitting delays will occur? He assigned scores in each dimension to the FM, and continued the process with his deputy for all FMs.

5. Multiply the three scores for each FM to arrive at a Composite score. For example, for the FM Permitting delays, DC estimated the scores in Severity, Probability and Detection to be 1, 2, and 1 respectively. Therefore, the composite score for this FM was 2.

Part of the table from Chapter G is reproduced below.

DIMENSION OF RISK	Permitting Delays	Constr Del
SEVERITY	1	2
PROBABILITY	2	1
DETECTION	1	1
COMPOSITE SCORE	2	2

NOTE: This is an abbreviated version of FMEA, and is adapted for use in personal life.

ACKNOWLEDGEMENTS

Thanks for joining me on the journey to Do-Magic! What a pleasure and honor it has been to be associated with each one of you; I have learned so much and in so many different ways.

Alan Lakshminarayanan	Luis Tavarez Jr.
Alba Figueroa	Mason Chen
Ashok Dhingra	Meeta Chowdhary
Ashok Khandkar	MyLin Lam
Aura Stewart	Nick Baguley
Bruce Brierly	Prabhakar Thirugnanasambandam
Chirag Gupta	Pradeep Dilwali
Chitra Gupta	Praful Mehta
Christin Choma	Prashant Dilwali
Diane Kimura	Pujeeta Chowdhary
Erico Almeida	Rabindernath Trehan
Fred Lopez	Robert Villalobos
Hillary Koellner	Sagar Gupta
Jeff Duckworth	Sandeep Dilwali
Jodie Hickman	Sandra Hemmert
John Acosta	Skyler Godfrey
Jon Samborski	Stacy Dymalski
Karan Jain	Steve Potts
Kevin Jessing	Sudhir Gupta
Lauren Nadler	Sushil Kohli
Layne Orr	Tyler Thorn

Made in the USA
Charleston, SC
14 April 2015